STUDENT UNIT GUIDE

NEW EDITION

OCR AS Economics Unit F582

The National and International Economy

John Hearn

Arnold
Rezida

PHILIP ALLAN

Philip Allan Updates, an imprint of Hodder Education, an Hachette UK company, Market Place, Deddington, Oxfordshire OX15 0SE

Orders
Bookpoint Ltd, 130 Milton Park, Abingdon, Oxfordshire OX14 4SB
tel: 01235 827827
fax: 01235 400401
e-mail: education@bookpoint.co.uk
Lines are open 9.00 a.m.–5.00 p.m., Monday to Saturday, with a 24-hour message answering service. You can also order through the Philip Allan Updates website: www.philipallan.co.uk

© John Hearn 2012

ISBN 978-1-4441-7212-6

First printed 2012
Impression number 5 4 3
Year 2016 2015 2014

Cover photo: Ingram

Typeset by Integra Software Services Pvt. Ltd., Pondicherry, India

Printed in Dubai

Hachette UK's policy is to use papers that are natural, renewable and recyclable products and made from wood grown in sustainable forests. The logging and manufacturing processes are expected to conform to the environmental regulations of the country of origin.

P2094

Contents

Content Guidance

Questions and Answers

Getting the most from this book

Examiner tips
Advice from the examiner on key points in the text to help you learn and recall unit content, avoid pitfalls, and polish your exam technique in order to boost your grade.

Knowledge check
Rapid-fire questions throughout the Content Guidance section to check your understanding.

Knowledge check answers

1 Turn to the back of the book for the Knowledge check answers.

Summary

Summaries

● Each core topic is rounded off by a bullet-list summary for quick-check reference of what you need to know.

Questions & Answers

Exam-style questions

Examiner comments on the questions
Tips on what you need to do to gain full marks, indicated by the icon **e**.

Sample student answers
Practise the questions, then look at the student answers that follow each set of questions.

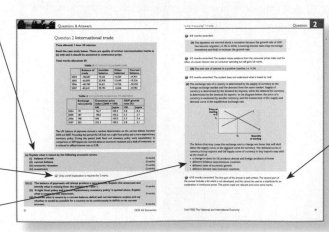

Examiner commentary on sample student answers
Find out how many marks each answer would be awarded in the exam and then read the examiner comments (preceded by the icon **e**) following each student answer.

About this book

'The National and International Economy' (Unit F582) is one of two compulsory units you will study in order to complete the AS specification in economics. It is probably the second unit you have studied in the first year of A-levels after 'Markets in Action' (Unit F581). Each of these two units accounts for 50% of the total AS mark. 'The National and International Economy' is also an important foundation for the final compulsory A2 unit 'The Global Economy' (Unit F585).

An understanding of governments' macroeconomic objectives and the techniques used to reach targets is important in this unit. When establishing policy, forecasting plays an important part in decision-making, so students need to be aware of the strengths and weaknesses of both creating and using forecasts. Remember that forecasts are not facts — there are no facts about the future.

Throughout this unit, the most important model you must learn to use is the aggregate supply/aggregate demand (*AS/AD*) model. It can be used to illustrate what may happen to the economy when either demand-side or supply-side policies are employed in macroeconomic management.

As soon as possible, you need to familiarise yourself with statistics and forecasts similar to those that are likely to be used in the examination. The internet provides a range of websites from which information can be gathered. Any search engine from an internet service provider can be a useful starting point. For example, type in 'inflation' or 'unemployment' and follow the options that are made available on-screen. Some useful websites are listed below:

- **www.statistics.gov.uk**
- **www.bankofengland.co.uk**
- **www.hm-treasury.gov.uk/press**
- **www.ecb.int** (European Central Bank)
- **www.worldbank.org** (for worldwide data and maps)
- **www.census.gov/main/www/stat_int.html** (a list of international agencies that provide statistics)
- **www.un.org** (and search for 'Cyberschoolbus' and 'InfoNation' among a choice of other useful sites)

How to use this guide

The guide is divided into two main sections to make your revision easier.

The **Content Guidance** section offers an overview of 'The National and International Economy' and covers three main areas of study:
- aggregate demand and aggregate supply and their interaction
- government economic policy objectives and indicators of national economic performance
- the application of macroeconomic policy instruments and the international economy

For each study area, there is a clear statement regarding the skills that must be developed. By the time of the examination, you must have learnt the definitions of

a number of key words and be able to understand certain concepts, hypotheses and theories. However, understanding is not enough and this part of the Unit Guide also highlights the things you need to be able to explain, analyse, apply and evaluate in the way required for the award of a high grade.

The **Questions and Answers** section includes six mock examinations which are subdivided into a case study and questions, followed by a mark scheme and two answers to A-grade and C-grade standards. The best way to use this section is as part of an intensive revision programme towards the end of the course. The reason for this is that each case study includes a range of questions that are spread across the whole specification and it would be counter-productive to test yourself on things you have not yet learnt. Below is a list of recommendations for using the case study questions and answers.

(1) During the early stages of the course, it may be useful to read through the questions only, without reference to the case study itself. This will provide a focus for the work you are doing and help you identify the things you will need to master before you can sit the examination with confidence.

(2) Towards the end of the course, find time to complete one or two case studies unseen, but also untimed. Then use the mark scheme to guide you through marking your own script. This is a useful exercise, because giving yourself the examiner's job can focus your attention on what is and what is not important. It is quality and not quantity that counts. A rough guide to the marks associated with each grade is as follows:

Grade A	80%+
Grade B	70–79%
Grade C	60–69%
Grade D	50–59%
Grade E	40–49%

Once you have marked your own answers, compare them with the A-grade and C-grade answers.

(3) At the end of the course — or with approximately 1 month to go before the examination — plan to intersperse the remaining four questions into your final revision programme. This time, observe strictly the examination timings so that you familiarise yourself with how much can be achieved in 1 hour 30 minutes. Be guided in the time you spend on the questions by the mark allocation at the end of each question and its subdivisions (e.g. if there are 90 minutes in which to achieve 60 marks, each mark is worth 1 minute 30 seconds of your precious time).

(4) When you look through the A-grade and C-grade answers, read carefully any comments that appear after the mark given to each sub-question. These comments offer useful hints and will help you avoid the all-too-common mistakes made by the unprepared examination student.

Planning your work and preparing a revision strategy

- Get hold of a copy of the specification and plan a structure into which to fit your notes.

- Make sure you compile notes on the whole specification. Do not leave any gaps because all questions in the examination are compulsory. It is therefore not possible to be selective without taking unnecessary risks.
- When you take notes from relevant material, try to put them into your own words. This process helps to develop and organise thoughts and is therefore much more useful than just copying your notes verbatim.
- Summarise when taking notes and use a highlighter pen to emphasise key points and help you focus your attention.
- Always ask yourself if your notes will make sense in 3 months' time.
- Whenever a planned or unplanned opportunity arises to practise the higher-level skills, take it — even if it means talking to yourself or arguing with other members of the family. In the examination, the requirement to use higher-level skills in your answer will usually be indicated in the question by the following words:
  - Analyse...
  - Elucidate...
  - Examine...
  - Explain why...

  while evaluation will be indicated by:
  - Evaluate...
  - Discuss...
  - Comment...
  - To what extent...?
  - Do you agree...?
- As early as possible, identify the dates of your examination(s) so that you can prepare a revision strategy. You should include a portion of time that can be used if any emergency should arise.
- Avoid the tendency to revise the material you already know and ignore the more difficult parts of the course. It is reasonable to assume that the aspects you fi... difficult are going to appear in the examination as a test of higher-level skills.
- The process of organisation, preparation and revision that goes on throughout the year will have rooted some content firmly in your long-term memory. ...ver the last few weeks, help your short-term memory to upload the final deta... by using acronyms to remember lists, patterns to remember links, and key w... ...s to trigger a series of associated points.

Content Guidance

This section outlines the topic areas of Unit F582, which are as follows:

- Aggregate demand and aggregate supply and their interaction.
- Government economic policy objectives and indicators of national economic performance.
- The application of macroeconomic policy instruments and the international economy.

Aggregate demand and aggregate supply and their interaction

This requires you to understand the components that make up aggregate demand and aggregate supply and the factors which influence their size and performance. In the same way that supply and demand analysis could be used to explain one market, their aggregated versions can be used to illustrate success and failure in achieving macroeconomic objectives.

Government economic policy objectives and indicators of national economic performance

The balance of supply and demand at the aggregate level would ideally produce full employment, stability in the average level of prices, equilibrium on the balance of payments and sustainable economic growth. These are the government's macro-economic objectives. The success of government in achieving these targets requires sound statistical measures of the state of the economy and how it is performing.

The application of macroeconomic policy instruments and the international economy

In order to achieve its macroeconomic objectives, the government has a variety of instruments at its disposal. To manipulate the demand side of the economy it can use monetary, fiscal and exchange rate policies, while an assortment of economic policies can be aggregated to boost the supply side of the economy.

The process of economic management can produce conflicts. For example, the objective of slowing inflation may improve the balance of payments, but worsen the level of employment and thereby slow economic growth.

Although much of the course content concentrates on the national economy, there is a long history of international trade between the UK and the rest of the world. This part of the course looks at why trade takes place and studies the costs and benefits of free and protected trade in international markets.

Aggregate demand and aggregate supply and their interaction

In Unit F581 'Markets in Action' you will have studied the way in which markets are analysed using supply and demand curves to produce equilibrium prices and output conditions. In this part of the course you are looking at the economy as if it was one big marketplace. All the individual market demand curves are added together to produce an aggregate demand curve and all the market supply curves are used to produce an aggregate supply curve.

The aggregate demand curve slopes down from left to right, meaning that if the average level of prices falls, then demand increases and vice versa. The components of aggregate demand (AD) in an economy are usually divided into:
- consumer expenditure (C)
- investment expenditure (I)
- government expenditure (G)
- export expenditure minus import expenditure (X – M)

This is symbolised as $AD = C + I + G + X - M$.

The aggregate demand curve can shift to the left or right, if more or fewer products are demanded at the same average level of prices. This may occur as a result of a change in any of the determinants of consumption, investment, government spending or imports and exports.

The aggregate supply curve slopes upwards from left to right on the assumption that firms expand their output as prices rise and potential profits increase. Aggregate supply is dependent upon changes in the conditions for supplying products.

For example, an improvement in technology may shift the curve to the right, while an increase in factor costs may shift it to the left. The slope of the aggregate supply curve varies, dependent upon the underlying assumptions used in its construction.

The normal aggregate supply curve (AS) is illustrated in Figure 1 (a). At the extreme are theories that support either a curve which is perfectly inelastic (AS_1) at the given level of employed resources, as in Figure 1 (b), or a curve which is assumed to be perfectly elastic if the economy has unemployed resources to the point when all resources are fully employed, where it becomes perfectly inelastic (AS_2). This is illustrated in Figure 1 (c).

Macroeconomic equilibrium is illustrated by the intersection of the aggregate demand curve (AD) and aggregate supply curve (AS), as illustrated in Figure 2.

As with the market analysis developed in Unit F581 'Markets in Action', a shift in one curve causes a movement along the other. In this component of Unit F582, it is necessary to understand the circular flow of income. This is determined by the propensity to consume plus the injections of income into the flow that increase its value and the leakages (withdrawals) from the flow that have a reducing effect.

Knowledge check 1

Identify three factors that will shift an aggregate supply curve to the right.

Examiner tip

The AD curve is always downward sloping from left to right, but the AS curve varies dependent upon how flexible or inflexible the real GDP is to shifts in aggregate demand.

Real/nominal GDP

Real GDP is a measure of the output of an economy usually over 1 year. Nominal GDP is the monetary value of this output. Therefore it is possible for nominal GDP to rise because of inflatio while real GDP remains unchanged.

Knowledge check 2

In Figure 1, is (a) or (b) most likely to be representative of a long-run situation?

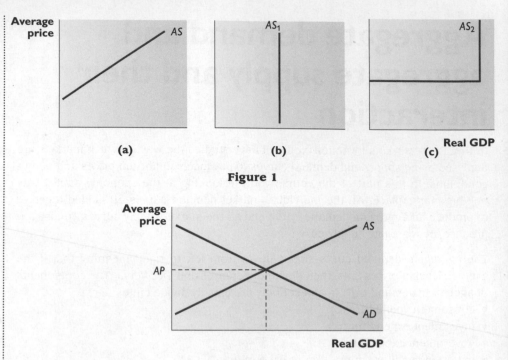

Figure 1

Figure 2

The main injections (J) and withdrawals (W) that affect the circular flow of income are paired into:

Injections	Withdrawals
investment (I)	savings (S)
government expenditure (G)	taxation (T)
exports (X)	imports (M)

Examiner tip

Do not refer to consumption as an injection into the circular flow of income. Consumption is a permanent flow and does not enter or leave the circular flow.

Any change in the value of injections into or withdrawals from the circular flow of income have an effect which is greater than the original change. This is because income flows from one economic unit to another, and the difference between the final change in GDP and the original change in withdrawals or injections is measured by the multiplier.

Essential terms

You will need to be able to define the following essential terms:

- aggregate demand curve
- aggregate supply curve
- consumer expenditure
- exports
- general equilibrium
- government expenditure
- imports
- injections
- investment
- multiplier
- savings
- taxation
- withdrawal (leakage)

Knowledge check 3

e the two main conomic policies e used to shift e supply curve.

9

Understanding

You will need to understand the following:

- How the market mechanism allocates resources.
- That many markets in the economy exist with or without government intervention and how policies can be pursued that affect the whole economy, rather than any particular market within the economy.
- The difference between microeconomics and macroeconomics.

Explanation

You will need to be able to explain the following:

- Why the aggregate demand curve slopes downward from left to right, the normal aggregate supply curve and the extreme cases.
- The *AS/AD* model and what is meant by general equilibrium in terms of output and the average level of prices.
- The **circular flow of income** and the multiplier effect of injections into and withdrawals from the flow.

Analysis

You will need to be able to analyse the following:

- The shifts and movements in the aggregate demand and aggregate supply curves.
- How the general equilibrium position is affected by changes in the conditions of aggregate demand and aggregate supply.

Evaluation

You will need to be able to evaluate the usefulness of *AD* and *AS* models in understanding the main macroeconomic models in an economy.

Check points

- Remember that you can apply the logic learnt under supply, demand and markets to aggregate supply, aggregate demand and general equilibrium in a market economy.
- A *shift in* an aggregate demand or aggregate supply curve occurs when more or less is demanded or supplied at the same average level of prices, while a *movement along* a curve occurs when the average level of prices changes.

Circular flow of income In this, the marginal propensity to consume is the proportion of additional income that will be used to consume domestic goods and services when income changes. It is positively related to the value of the multiplier in as much as a high marginal propensity to consume will bring about a higher value for the multiplier.

- In your mind, clearly separate factors that cause the *AD* and *AS* curves to shift and those that cause a movement along the curve.
- Aggregate demand curves always slope downward from left to right. For aggregate supply curves there are a variety of slopes that depend upon the theories that underpin them.
- An injection into, or a leakage from, the circular flow of income will usually change the GDP, real or nominal, by more than the value of the injection/leakage such that:

$$\frac{\text{change in GDP}}{\text{change in injection/leakage}} = \text{value of the multiplier}$$

- When discussing outward shifts in the *AD* curve, theories which assume that an economy can settle at less than maximum capacity output predict output and employment can increase, while those that assume that an economy has a vertical *AS* curve predict inflation.

Summary

Government economic policy objectives and indicators of national economic performance

The indicators of national economic performance over the last 100 years have — even if we exclude exceptional periods like 1914–18 and 1939–45 — shown significant yearly variations, such as:

- the average level of prices falling by 10% in 1920 and rising by 30% in 1976
- the percentage of the workforce unemployed fluctuating from a high of 22% in 1932 to a low of 0.9% in 1955
- the balance of payments current account ranging between a deficit of £29 billion in 2011 to a £6 billion surplus in 1997
- economic growth rates ranging from –1.6% in 1975 to +5.2% in 1988

Examiner tip

Since 2009 there has been the threat of deflation and recession. Deflation, as a fall in the average level of prices, has been avoided as the result of the Bank of England's quantitative easing programme which injected £200 billion of new money into the economy followed by a further £75 billion in 2011 and £50 billion in 2012.

A 30% rate of inflation — coupled with high negative real rates of interest — creates significant redistributions of income and wealth and particularly hurts those people who live off their savings or who receive fixed incomes. When 22% of the workforce is unemployed this creates poverty, reduces living standards, provokes social and industrial unrest and increases crime rates. It is not only the person who loses a job that is affected. Anyone who relies in whole or in part on his or her income is also affected. Large fluctuations in the current account of the balance of payments can have significant distorting effects on the external rate of exchange and the prices of imports and exports. Growth rates of 5% create expectations that standards of living are growing fast and when these do not materialise — as the growth rate becomes negative — this can have distorting effects on wage claims and expenditure plans. The variations described are dependent upon the reliability of the statistical techniques used to measure them.

Inflation rates were calculated from changes in the retail price index (RPI, which is known as the headline rate of inflation and RPIX, which excludes mortgage interest rates and is known as the underlying rate of inflation). Because of the immense task involved, the RPI cannot take account of all the price changes that take place in an economy over a given period of time. Instead, a shopping basket of representative products — chosen to reflect the average family — is measured. If you are not average, then these changes may not reflect the way that the value of the money you spend has changed. Although the RPI calculations are still used for certain things such as index linking, they are not now the primary measure of inflation. This is carried out by the consumer price index (CPI) which was introduced to conform to the Eurozone measure, the harmonised index of consumer prices (HICP). The core CPI excludes the cost of volatile items such as energy and food. In the UK the year-on-year measure of inflation in January 2008 by the RPI was 4.1% and by the CPI was 2.1%. This difference has fuelled a debate over which is the truer measure of inflation.

Measures of unemployment may be significantly different from the number of people who are available to contribute to the productive process but are not currently doing so. Over the years, governments have been astute at finding ways of removing people from the unemployment register. While this reduces the number counted as unemployed in official statistics, it does not necessarily mean that there are fewer people looking for work. Unemployment is measured by the Claimant Count, which is a total measure of those claiming unemployment benefits, and the International Labour Organisation (ILO) unemployment rate (Labour Force Survey), which is estimated from a sample and includes those available, willing, looking and in the process of changing jobs.

Errors and omissions in the **balance of payments** statistics require balancing items to produce an accounting equality. In addition, the demand for statistics to be produced as quickly as possible sometimes means that revised figures provided at a later date can show significant changes.

The growth rate of the economy is most commonly accounted for using gross domestic product (GDP). This can be measured in any of three ways:
- income
- output
- expenditure

Whichever measure is used, each one creates problems and although, in theory, they should produce the same total over the same period of time, this never happens in practice. Once again, estimates have to be used to cover statistical errors and omissions.

Finally, it is necessary to recognise the possibility of conflicting outcomes from the pursuit of a specific objective. For example, an attempt to boost **economic growth** may result in a rise in the rate of inflation and a worsening of the balance on current account.

Essential terms

You will need to be able to define the following essential terms:
- aggregate demand
- aggregate supply
- balance of payments
- circular flow of income
- demand management
- economic growth
- exchange rates
- fiscal policy
- gross domestic product
- inflation
- macroeconomics
- monetary policy
- nominal
- real
- supply-side economics
- unemployment

Understanding

You will need to understand the following:
- What is meant by the macroeconomic policy objectives of government and how these differ from other policies that are targeted at a particular sector of the economy.

Balance of payments
The difference between the total payments into and out of a country, measured in domestic currency over a given period of time.

Examiner tip
An economy can grow by utilising previously unused resources in it. This means the economy is moving closer to its productive possibility boundary. This is different from economic growth that shifts the production possibility boundary outwards.

Economic growth This results from a per capita increase in the productive capacity of an economy.

Knowledge check 4

If a government aims to boost employment by expanding aggregate monetary demand, which two macroeconomic targets may be compromised?

- The reason why government establishes such objectives, and the policy options available to achieve these goals.
- The difference between monetary policy (which targets the money supply and interest rates); fiscal policy (which uses the government's budget); exchange rate policy (which changes the external value of the currency); and supply-side policies (which aim to boost output and productivity).
- The difference between nominal and real in measuring and valuing an economy. There must also be a recognition that the nominal and the real can move in opposite directions, as illustrated by a nominal rise in GDP, which is less than the rate of inflation, leading to a fall in real GDP.

Explanation

You will need to be able to explain the following:

- The four main government objectives of persistently low inflation, low levels of unemployment, long-term balance of payments equilibrium and sustainable economic growth.
- Different rates of inflation, the difference between accelerating and stable inflation, and between anticipated and unanticipated inflation.
- The various measures of employment and unemployment.
- The structure of the balance of payments, including the various components of the current account, the financial account (formerly known as the capital account) and the new capital account, which includes only transactions in fixed assets. You will also need to explain the effect that changes in the balance of payments have on the exchange rate and vice versa.
- How economic growth is measured, the costs and benefits of economic growth and the advantages of sustainable growth.
- The three ways of measuring economic performance, i.e. income, output and expenditure, and the problems of getting the right information and making the correct interpretation.
- The use of index numbers to represent changes in economic performance and the method of calculating the retail price index and the consumer price index.

Examiner tip

It is easier to remember the costs of economic growth if you group them as follows:

- the opportunity cost in terms of a reduction in potential current consumption
- the individual cost as people have to adjust to continually changing conditions of employment
- the external costs in terms of various types of pollution

Analysis

You will need to be able to analyse the following:

- The trends and breaks in trend for all the key economic indicators, i.e. inflation, unemployment, balance of payments, economic growth and GDP.
- Comparisons of economic performance between countries using the relevant data sets.
- The effect on the economy of changes to fiscal, monetary, exchange rate and supply-side policies. You will also need to show awareness of how changes in one policy may affect another, e.g. changes in fiscal policy will affect monetary policy.

Knowledge check 5

Give some examples of supply-side policies.

Evaluation

You will need to be able to evaluate the following:

- The consequences for the economy of high rates of unemployment, high and accelerating inflation, balance of payments disequilibrium and slow or negative economic growth.

- The potential for conflict as government tries to pursue multiple policy targets, and the trade-offs that have to be made, e.g. a boost to economic growth damages the balance of payments.
- The macroeconomic policy objectives of government in terms of their expected outcome and their actual outcome, e.g. is there a conflict between quality of life and faster economic growth?

Check points

Be aware of the following points:

- Remember that there is considerable disagreement among those economists who insist that economic management is best pursued through demand-side policies and those who support the use of supply-side policies.
- If the government pursued an expansionary fiscal policy by budgeting for a deficit, this is likely to change monetary conditions, as interest rates may have to be raised to finance the debt or the government's cash requirement may increase.
- The continued existence of macroeconomic problems suggests that governments do not have all the answers and may, through their actions, make problems worse rather than better.

Examiner tip

Since 2009 a worldwide recession and economic crises in banking and the euro have forced governments into using expansionary demand management policies:

- Fiscal policy has resulted in large budget deficits.
- Monetary policy has resulted in bank rates that have fallen as far as they can go (0.5% in the UK) and a quantitative easing programme to stimulate monetary expansion.

Summary

- Be aware of the possible conflict caused by macroeconomic targeting. If the government uses expansionary policies then this may benefit growth and employment but may damage the external account and inflation; vice versa for a contractionary policy.
- There are some economists who do not see the conflict described above. They argue that a stable low inflation target is sufficient to create the best economic environment for economic growth to flourish, employment to improve and a satisfactory balance of payments to prevail.
- A major problem that government has is that it bases its financial decisions on what is happening now and what is expected to happen in the future. For example, if it assumed that real GDP will grow by 3% next year it may then plan to spend more money based on that assumption and subsequently be caught out if that rate of growth does not materialise.
- Supply-side economists do not see a solution to the main macroeconomic problems through adjustments to aggregate demand. They want attention focused on the factors that inhibit the efficient allocation of resources and the application of policies designed to eliminate these constraints.

The application of macroeconomic policy instruments and the international economy

In macroeconomic management there is a broad division between those policies that target the demand side of the economy and those that target the supply side. Fiscal and monetary policies aim to boost or suppress aggregate monetary demand. Supply-side policies focus on specific problems and solutions, including making labour markets more efficient through improved training and education, the creation of incentives to work harder and the reform of trade union law. Privatisation and deregulation have been used to encourage more competition.

Fiscal policy uses the balance between government expenditure and taxation to manipulate aggregate demand. More spending and/or less taxation produces an expansionary fiscal policy, while a contractionary policy involves more taxation and/or less spending.

Monetary policy is concerned with adjustments to the supply of money in the economy and changes in the rate of interest. These can occur together or can be pursued independently, but even then it is not possible to separate the effects that interest rates have on the money supply and vice versa. Until recently the Bank of England used interest rates to control aggregate monetary demand, but after the **credit crunch** of 2008/09 the lowering of the Bank of England's base rate to 0.5% had little effect on boosting demand so it introduced a programme of quantitative easing to expand the quantity of money (cash) in the economy. £200 billion was used to buy back mainly government debt and expand the economy's liquidity. In 2011 a further £75 billion was added to the economy and in 2012 a further £50 billion.

Exchange rates are determined by supply and demand, and governments may intervene in the buying and selling of currency to pursue an exchange rate policy as part of their macroeconomic management.

The policies described above can be used separately or in combination to shift the aggregate demand and/or aggregate supply curves to a new position dependent upon which policy target has priority.

- To lower unemployment, expansionary fiscal and/or monetary policies shift the *AD* curve to the right. Over the longer term, supply-side policies could be used to shift the *AS* curve to the right.
- To lower inflation, contractionary fiscal and monetary policies could be used to remove the excessive monetary demand. Over the longer term, supply-side policies could be used to boost output, shift the *AS* curve to the right and absorb the excessive monetary demand.

Credit crunch This occurs when banks reduce lending, usually because of some unexpected event that shocks financial markets. In 2008/09 it was the problem of sub-prime lending in US mortgages and the collapse of Lehman Brothers.

Knowledge check 6

What is an expansionary fiscal policy?

- To remove a balance of payments current account deficit, contractionary fiscal and monetary policies could be used or exchange rates lowered. Over the longer term, supply-side policies could be used to promote exports and reduce imports.
- To promote economic growth, supply-side policies designed to boost productivity and improve technology could be pursued.

A closed economy is one that does not trade with other countries. The UK is an open economy, exporting between one-fifth and one-quarter of its gross domestic product and importing a similar amount. Since the UK joined the European Economic Community (EEC) in 1973, the pattern of trade has shifted from its Commonwealth partner countries to the other members of what is now termed the European Union (EU). Over the same period, there has been a decline in the proportion of goods relative to services that are exported from the UK.

The theories of absolute advantage and comparative advantage explain not only the benefits of internal trade, but also those of international trade. Adam Smith (1723–90) explained the trade gains that occur when one country has an absolute advantage in the production of some products and trades with other countries which have an absolute advantage in the production of other products. David Ricardo (1772–1823) went one stage further and showed that there can still be gains from trade even if a country has an absolute disadvantage in the production of all products, so long as it has lower opportunity costs of production and therefore a comparative advantage in the production of some products.

The main difference between internal trade and international trade is that internal trade is usually conducted in one currency and is relatively free from trade restrictions, whereas international trade is made more difficult by the need to trade currencies as well as products, and the degree to which countries protect themselves using options such as:

- tariffs
- quotas
- subsidies to domestic industry
- legislation
- quality control
- differential tax rates

The case for protectionism includes a variety of more or less sound economic arguments including:

- the protection of infant industries
- the protection of senile industries to allow them time to regenerate
- the countering of unfair trading practices such as **dumping**
- protection against illegal imports
- the protection of employment in industries sensitive to foreign competition
- a source of revenue for government

The case against protectionism includes:

- the advantages of free trade
- the problem that infant industries may never grow up and therefore may not be able to compete

> **Examiner tip**
> When explaining gains from trade always use an example of a country that has absolute advantage in the production of both products, but a comparative advantage in one product (opportunity costs are different). This clearly illustrates that you understand the concept.

> **Dumping** This involves offering a product for sale in another country at a loss-making price below its cost of production. It may be to break into a new market, to sell off a surplus that cannot be cleared in the home market, or to generate an inflow of foreign currency.

- the fact that protecting an inefficient industry while it regenerates can lead to a permanent rather than temporary misallocation of resources
- the retaliations other countries may impose
- the rise in the cost of living and the restriction of consumer choice

Since the Second World War, there has been a concerted effort to lower trade barriers throughout the world. When countries joined the EU, they accepted free trade within its boundaries plus a common external tariff determined by the member country which originally had the lowest tariff with the rest of the world. In addition, the General Agreement on Tariffs and Trade (GATT), which was established in 1948, aimed to reduce protectionist measures between all countries in the world. This work was taken over by the World Trade Organization (WTO) in 1995.

Essential terms

Examiner tip

Opportunity cost is important in the theory of comparative advantage: it not only identifies who has comparative advantage in which product but also shows the limits to exchange if both parties are to benefit from trade and indicates where the terms of trade will settle in a free market.

You will need to be able to define the following essential terms:

- absolute advantage
- balance of payments
- comparative advantage
- interest rates
- international trade
- money supply
- current account deficit
- deregulation
- dumping
- European Union
- free trade
- gains from trade
- infant industry
- opportunity cost
- privatisation
- protection
- quota
- tariff
- World Trade Organization

Understanding

You will need to understand the following:

- What is meant by fiscal policy, monetary policy, exchange rate policy and supply-side economics.
- The difference between demand management and supply-side management of the economy.
- That fiscal, monetary and exchange rate policies are all demand-side policies.
- The pattern of trade between the UK and the EU, and the UK and the rest of the world, including some historical perspective on the broad changes that have taken place over time.
- The importance of imports and exports to the health of the UK economy, including knowledge of the main types of products traded internationally.

Explanation

Knowledge check 7

What determines the supply of currency to the foreign exchange market?

You will need to be able to explain:

- How fiscal policy can be used to change aggregate demand.
- The relationship between interest rates, money supply and aggregate monetary demand.
- The determination of an exchange rate using supply and demand curves for currency.

- The determination of interest rates using supply and demand curves for money and/or supply of savings and demand for loans.
- The gains that economies can make through engaging in international trade. Brief reference may be made to absolute and comparative advantage, but it will not be necessary to produce numerical examples.
- The advantages of free trade as opposed to the resource misallocation that takes place behind trade barriers.
- The various tariff and non-tariff methods of protecting the domestic economy from potential problems caused by free international trade.

Examiner tip

There are two theories of interest rate determination: one is the Keynesian theory of liquidity preference which looks at the supply and demand for money; the second is loanable funds theory which looks at the supply of savings and the demand for loans in financial markets.

Analysis

You will need to be able to analyse the way in which demand-side and supply-side policies can be used to shift aggregate demand and aggregate supply curves and their effect on the average level of prices and real GDP.

You will need to be able to use supply and demand analysis to illustrate the various equilibriums that may exist in an economy, as illustrated in Figure 3.

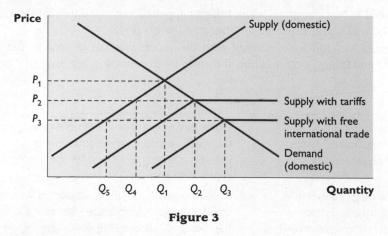

Figure 3

P_1Q_1 = no international trade

P_2Q_2 = trade behind a tariff barrier

P_3Q_3 = free trade

In the example, also note that domestic supply is Q_1 with no international trade and falls back to Q_4 with tariffs and Q_5 with free trade. Given international trade, the supply curves become perfectly elastic on the assumption that an infinite supply of imports can take place at a single price, i.e. P_3 with free trade and P_2 with an added tariff.

In addition to the above, you will need to be able to analyse the impact that membership of the European Union has had on the pattern of UK trade.

Knowledge check 8

In Figure 3 by how much does domestic supply change when there is free international trade compared to a domestic equilibrium?

Evaluation

You will need to be able to evaluate the likely success of the policies chosen to achieve the macroeconomic objectives, and the conflicts that need to be reconciled.

You will need to be able to evaluate the arguments for and against trading products freely throughout the world as opposed to the erection of trade barriers that are used to protect economies.

Check points

Be aware of the following:

- Do not confuse fiscal and monetary policy. Remember, fiscal policy is concerned with taxation and expenditure, and monetary policy with the money supply and interest rates.
- Do not confuse changes in the balance between total taxation and expenditure (which are part of macroeconomic demand management) with adjustments to individual taxes and particular areas of expenditure that are part of supply-side policy. For example, a reduction in higher marginal rates of tax may be an attempt to motivate the workforce, while increased expenditure on education and training is likely to be concerned with improving labour productivity. Neither need change the balance between taxation and expenditure and would therefore be supply-side policies.
- The need to be clear about when things happened, e.g. the date that the UK joined the EEC (1973) and when the EEC became the EU (1993).
- The need to familiarise yourself with the representation of data in the form of graphs and tables, as this is how they may be presented in the examination.

Knowledge check 9

(a) In which year did the Bank of England become independent?

(b) In which year did some members of the EU adopt the euro as their currency?

Summary

- Do not confuse the four macroeconomic policies identified in this section of the specification. Make sure you can clearly define and separate each from the other.

- Once you have a clear understanding of the difference between each policy make sure that you can identify the ways in which one policy may affect the others. For example, a fiscal policy with a large budget deficit may cause the money supply to expand or interest rates to rise.

- Use the *AD/AS* model to explain how different policies will shift and move along curves.

- Make sure you are able to show how different theorists, i.e. monetarists and Keynesians, assume different starting positions for the aggregate supply curve.

- The strongest argument in support of international trade is the gains from trade that are explained by the theory of comparative advantage. However, there are also strong economic arguments for protection in the case of dumping and infant industries.

Questions & Answers

How to use this section

In this section of the guide there are six questions, each followed by two sample answers interspersed with examiner's comments.

Questions

There are six case study examination papers which are constructed to reflect the AS format. The last question of each paper must be answered in continuous prose and includes marks for quality of written communication. The time allocated to reading the case study and answering the questions is 1 hour 30 minutes. The questions in each examination paper range across the entire AS specification for Unit F582. They test a hierarchy of skills, starting with definitions and basic understanding of 'The National and International Economy' and its specialised language, and progressing to include your ability to explain this knowledge. Beyond this, the higher-level skills of application, analysis and evaluation are tested. Each question is followed by a brief analysis of what to watch out for when answering it (shown by the symbol ⓮).

Mark schemes

These are similar to those an examiner would use to complete the initial marking of a script. Each scheme highlights the points that will score marks. However, they are for guidance and do not necessarily illustrate the only correct interpretation. Some answers may be different and equally valid and would therefore be awarded equal marks. The mark schemes are designed to help you to focus your attention on what the examiner is looking for in the award of marks. Do not be tempted to read these mark schemes before you attempt to answer the questions. Use these examination papers as if they were the real thing.

Sample answers and examiner comments

After each question and mark scheme there are two scripts that reflect the answers required for the award of a grade A and a grade C. The A-grade answers are not perfect, but are sufficient to achieve 80% or more, while the C-grade answers have some errors and omissions that cause them to score between 60 and 69%. Throughout the sample answers, examiner comments are included, preceded by the symbol ⓮. These comments reflect the strengths and weaknesses of answers, as well as pointing out common errors which have been made by many students in the past, but should not be made by you in the future.

Assessment objectives

Two broad skills are being assessed, which can be divided into:
- understanding
- expression

Assessment objectives	Skills	Percentage of total mark
Level 1	The ability to understand and express knowledge of the specification content, e.g. know that the government's macroeconomic objectives are a high level of employment, a sustained low rate of inflation, a satisfactory balance on external account and economic growth.	30%
Level 2	The ability to apply knowledge and understanding critically to the problems and issues that manifest themselves, e.g. understand the economic implications of high unemployment, accelerating inflation, balance of payments disequilibrium and negative economic growth.	30%
Level 3	The ability to use economic principles to analyse the problems and issues, e.g. use the *AS/AD* model to illustrate and analyse the main macroeconomic problems.	20%
Level 4	The ability to reflect upon economic arguments, evaluate evidence and make informed judgements as an economist, e.g. does solving one macroeconomic problem create conflicts with the policies used to solve the other problems, and if so how are the resulting trade-offs evaluated?	20%

Understanding

In some examinations, it has been possible for students to show an understanding of a subject and achieve a good mark on, say, a multiple-choice question paper but not be able to express that understanding clearly. Consequently, they achieve a relatively low mark on an essay paper. In this examination, however, there are no separate papers so you need to understand the subject and choose your words, numbers, formulae and diagrams carefully when answering the questions because this will determine your final mark. In addition to this, you are informed that one question will require you to write in continuous prose, and a proportion of the marks allocated to this question will test your ability to organise your thoughts and express them, using a form of writing that is appropriate to the question. Sentences must be legible with correct spelling, grammar and punctuation. This means that, if at the end of the examination you have time to check only one thing, make sure it is your answer to this last question.

Expression

The examining board separates the assessment objectives into four skill levels. These are illustrated in the table above by reference to the government's macroeconomic objectives. It is important to note that the assessment objectives for AS are weighted more heavily towards Levels 1 and 2, while the A2 papers that complete the A-level specification show a 30% weighting to Levels 3 and 4 and a 20% weighting to Levels 1 and 2.

Question 1 International economic comparisons

Time allowed: 1 hour 30 minutes

Read the case study below. There are quality of written communication marks in (e) only and it should be answered in continuous prose.

Total marks allocated: 60

Table 1 A comparison of the UK and Ethiopia

2010	GDP per capita ($)	GDP per capita (PPP$)	Human development index	External debt (% of GDP)
Ethiopia	351	1,092	0.328	124
UK	39,604	35,974	0.863	0

In order to compare the UK and Ethiopia, it is necessary to convert domestic currencies into a common currency. As the Ethiopian currency is not traded on the foreign exchange market, the official government rate is used. To make a clearer comparison of living standards, the United Nations International Comparison Project has produced an alternative set of exchange rates. These are measured as purchasing power parity figures (PPP$) and are illustrated in Table 1. They represent an attempt to equalise the spending power of each domestic currency.

Table 2 shows a comparison over 3 years of three key variables between the UK and USA.

Table 2 A comparison of the UK and USA (%)

	2005	2006	2007
UK			
Growth	3.7	2.5	2.1
Inflation/CPI	2.0	2.4	2.9
Interest rates	4.75	5.00	5.75
USA			
Growth	3.7	3.9	2.5
Inflation	1.8	2.1	2.3
Interest rates	4.25	4.5	4.25

(a) The following economic terms are used in the description. Explain what is meant by:

   (i) GDP per capita (2 marks)

   (ii) foreign exchange market (2 marks)

   (iii) interest rate (2 marks)

ℯ Each answer requires slightly more than just a definition of each term.

(b) (i) Explain why the GDP per capita in Ethiopia is considerably different when measured in US dollars compared with GDP per capita (PPP$), and why the UK GDP per capita totals are very similar. (4 marks)

(e) Search for a reason why the numbers are different for the UK and Ethiopia.

(ii) The human development index (HDI) is calculated using three criteria, only one of which relates to the spending power of a person's income. Choose any two additional criteria that you think should be included in a development index and explain your choice. (6 marks)

(e) You can make your own choice of criteria as long as you justify it.

(iii) Based on GDP per capita ($), what is the value of external debt per person in Ethiopia and in the UK? (2 marks)

(e) Make a calculation from the statistics.

(iv) In respect of interest rates, explain one disadvantage of having a large external debt. (2 marks)

(e) Relate your answer only to interest rates.

(c) (i) Given only the statistics in Table 2, explain why the growth rate in the USA is faster than in the UK. (6 marks)
(ii) Explain how the rate of inflation is calculated in the UK. (6 marks)

(e) Use either method for the second part.

(d) What are the problems of using GDP statistics to measure differences in living standards:
(i) over time in the same country? (5 marks)
(ii) at one point in time between countries? (5 marks)

(e) Some economic history is required to answer the first part, and a spatial comparison for the second part.

(e) Discuss the ways in which government can manage an economy to encourage economic growth. (18 marks)

(e) As it is a discussion, identify possible options and evaluate their effectiveness.

Mark scheme

(a) (i) A measure of the domestic output of an economy over a given period of time divided by the population (2 marks).

(ii) A market where foreign currencies are traded and the price is determined by the supply of and the demand for each individual currency (2 marks).

(iii) An interest rate is the cost of borrowing money, or the price of capital, or the reward for parting with liquidity (2 marks).

(b) (i) Look for an explanation of how a currency traded freely on the foreign exchange market will more closely reflect its purchasing power than a currency which is fixed by a government and not traded internationally (4 marks).

(ii) The two HDI criteria are (a) literacy and school enrolment and (b) life expectancy, but allow any two justified criteria (2 × 3 marks).

(iii) Ethiopia = $435.2 (1 mark), UK = $0 (1 mark).

(iv) May include the need to earn foreign currency to service the debt or the possible variations that take place in interest rates over time (2 marks).

(c) (i) It is necessary to identify the growth rates for the UK and USA, pointing out the faster rate of growth in the USA (2 marks). Identify the lower rates of inflation and explain the possible effect on growth (2 marks). Identify the lower rates of interest and explain the possible effect on growth (2 marks).

(ii) An explanation of the consumer price index or retail price index is sufficient and, in addition to the final calculation, should point out that:
- a representative basket of products is chosen
- each item is given the index number 100 in a base year
- each item is weighted dependent on the pattern of consumer expenditure
- percentage changes are added or taken away from the index number
  (6 marks)

(d) (i) Expect an answer which looks at the problems over time to include some of the following:
- population changes
- variations in statistical calculation
- changes in money value
- balance of payments disequilibriums
- distribution of income and wealth
- changes in working conditions
- exceptional years
- externalities
  (5 marks)

(ii) The problems between countries should include differences in some of the following:
- currencies
- methods of collection
- distribution of income and wealth
- non-marketed resources
- leisure time
- defence budgets
- externalities
  (5 marks)

(e) Expect an explanation of what is meant by economic growth and how the government can use its macroeconomic policies — including fiscal, monetary, exchange rate and supply side — to create an economic environment that will foster growth or be actively involved in trying to stimulate growth (14 marks + 4 marks for quality of written communication).

A-grade answer

(a) (i) GDP stands for gross domestic product, and it is a measure of the total output of any economy, usually measured over one year. This total is then divided by the number of people in the country to get a per capita figure.

(e) **2/2 marks awarded.**

(ii) The foreign exchange market is made up of many firms which buy and sell the currencies of the more developed countries. The price of a currency is established by the supply of currency (which is determined by the demand for imports) and the demand for currency (which is determined by the demand for exports).

(e) **2/2 marks awarded.** This is an excellent answer, although perhaps it goes into more detail than is required to achieve full marks.

(iii) The rate of interest is what is charged to a borrower for a loan and what is paid to a saver to compensate for parting with liquidity. It is usually referred to as a rate per annum.

(e) **2/2 marks awarded.**

(b) (i) If the Ethiopian currency is not traded on foreign exchange markets, then people who travel to Ethiopia will probably have to buy domestic currency at a rate fixed by the government. It is likely, in the case of Ethiopia, that this rate is significantly different from a rate that would reflect the buying power of the currency. In contrast, in the UK, sterling is traded on the foreign exchange market and it is likely that the market rate will reflect the buying power of the currency; otherwise there would be a significant distortion in the price of UK products in foreign markets and vice versa.

(e) **4/4 marks awarded.**

(ii) The life expectancy and proportion of children surviving until the age of five can indicate a more or less advanced country.

(e) **2/6 marks awarded.** The student identifies two relevant criteria but does not offer an explanation of either.

(iii) Ethiopia — external debt is 124% of 351 = $435.2
UK — external debt is 0% of 39,604 = $0

(e) **2/2 marks awarded.**

(iv) A large external debt means that a country will have to sell products abroad to earn the foreign currency to finance this debt.

(e) **2/2 marks awarded.**

(c) (i) The growth rate in the USA may be faster because the interest rate is lower and therefore there will be more investment. Also, inflation is lower and this creates a more stable economic environment.

ⓔ 4/6 marks awarded. The student identifies that interest rates are lower and that this could lead to more investment (2 marks) and also that inflation is lower and this will cause more stability (2 marks). These points would need to be expanded for a higher mark.

> **(ii)** In the UK, inflation can be measured by using the retail price index, although the official government measure is now the CPI. The RPI selects 600 items and asks approximately 7,000 households to keep a record of the price paid for these items and how much is spent on them. Each item is given a base number and weights are allocated to the item dependent on the proportion spent by consumers. Percentage changes in price are added to or taken away from the index number and a new retail price average index is calculated by multiplying each index number by its weight, then adding up the new index number for each item and dividing by the number of weights.

ⓔ 6/6 marks awarded.

> **(d) (i)** The statistics for gross domestic product have not always been available and therefore they can only be used to compare changes over time in the same country relatively recently. Also, the size of the population has changed, so GDP figures only become meaningful if they are per capita figures.
>
> Over time the quality and range of products purchased has changed and this will alter living standards, but is not reflected in raw figures.
>
> Inflation means that nominal figures are meaningless and a GDP deflator will have to be used so that the statistics reflect real changes in GDP.
>
> Over the years, there will have been changes in working conditions and working practices which will have improved life at work as well as increasing the number of leisure hours and reducing working hours. These changes will not have been registered in higher incomes, but they will have increased standards of living.

ⓔ 4/5 marks awarded.

> **(ii)** Between countries there must be an adjustment to a common currency in order to make comparisons. Also, there is a difficulty to overcome where exchange rates do not reflect purchasing power in each country.
>
> From one country to another the methods of collecting statistics vary, with different countries relying on sampling to a greater or lesser extent. Also, non-marketed products will vary from one country to another. In Singapore, it is not necessary to spend money on heating, whereas it commands a significant amount of expenditure in Iceland.
>
> Defence budgets vary from one country to another and the larger the proportion of GDP spent on defence, the lower the living standards.

ⓔ 4/5 marks awarded.

(e) There are various and conflicting views about how the government can manage an economy to encourage economic growth.

At one extreme there is a non-interventionist view that suggests government should create a stable framework of rules within which a competitive capitalist economy can produce the necessary motivation for it to grow. Monetary policy needs to be focused on creating price stability with a current official target of 2% inflation, while exchange rate policy can be aimed at keeping the value of the currency stable in international foreign exchange markets. Fiscal policy can be used to support the monetary and exchange rate policies and the government should focus on their golden rule and sustainable investment rule to ensure that their finances do not crowd out private sector initiatives to carry out the investment that is necessary to bring about economic growth.

At the other extreme is a view that, left to its own devices, a capitalist economy will be sluggish and businessmen will shrug off risk to pursue the quiet life. In this situation, the government must be proactive. It should use its fiscal policy to kick-start the economy whenever it is tending towards recession by budgeting for a deficit and expanding aggregate monetary demand.

In order to increase the economy's productive capacity, the government may use its expenditure directly to invest in new social and industrial capital. Exchange rate policy may be used to keep export prices competitive and this may involve allowing the exchange rate to depreciate so that export prices fall and import prices rise, making domestic producers most competitive.

Finally, the government must make monetary policy responsive to the demands of fiscal policy and it should not impose constraints on the way in which fiscal policy is used to manage the economy.

The current view of government policy is that the economy should be stable in terms of prices and the exchange rate and that, within this environment, competitive forces will help promote growth. It is not expected that government will use demand management policies, but that it should use supply-side policies to ensure that sustainable economic growth is achieved. This means promoting a level playing field and ensuring that there is a fostering of competition among firms competing for their share of the market.

ⓔ 14/18 marks awarded. The answer is well balanced and a good attempt at discussion. It is also well written and achieves maximum marks for written communication.

ⓔ Scored 48/60   80% = Grade A

C-grade answer

(a)   (i) GDP per capita is gross domestic product per person.

ⓔ 1/2 marks awarded. The student says what the term is, but offers no explanation.

(ii) The foreign exchange market is where different currencies are bought and sold.

e **1/2 marks awarded.** The student offers limited explanation.

> **(iii)** The interest rate is the price that has to be paid for taking out a loan.

e **1/2 marks awarded.** The student gives limited coverage.

> **(b)** **(i)** In Ethiopia, the gross domestic product per capita measured in terms of dollars is a small fraction of the GDP figure for the UK. However, when it is measured in terms of the purchasing power of each domestic currency, it is a much higher fraction of the UK figure. This means that the people in Ethiopia are significantly better off using the PPP$ calculation than is implied by the raw exchange rate. This may be because the government is intervening in the market for foreign currency.

e **3/4 marks awarded.** This reasonable attempt at an answer loses a mark through not referring to the use of an official government rate in Ethiopia.

> **(ii)** Life expectancy varies considerably from the more developed to the less developed countries, where the average age of death can be in the 30s. As people's real income rises, so they buy cars and therefore a calculation of population size divided by the number of cars in a country would indicate how far they had developed.

e **6/6 marks awarded.**

> **(iii)** $435.2 in Ethiopia and zero in the UK.

e **2/2 marks awarded.**

> **(iv)** Over time, interest rates can rise and fall considerably so that a country with a large external debt will have to pay large variable payments to service the debt.

e **2/2 marks awarded.**

> **(c)** **(i)** The growth rate in the UK was lower than the USA because the rate of inflation was higher and the interest rate in two out of the three years was higher. A higher interest rate is likely to mean less consumer demand in the UK, and a higher rate of inflation may have been caused by a rise in the costs of production which has made the UK economy less competitive.

e **3/6 marks awarded.** The answer does not consider the benefits of lower rates for inflation and interest in the USA.

(ii) It is usual to measure the rate of inflation using the retail price index (RPI). The RPI is calculated using a basket of products which are consumed by the average family. Percentage changes in prices and weights are added to each product and then an average for all the products in the basket is calculated.

ⓔ 3/6 marks awarded. The description is too brief and there is some uncertainty over the way in which weights are used in the index.

(d) (i) Over time the ways in which GDP statistics have been collected have varied, as has the size of the population, and this would need to be taken into account when using the statistics to measure living standards. Also it is important to make sure that a real measure of GDP is used to adjust inflationary changes to the nominal figures. It is also important to remember that living standards are comprised of more things than just money measures, and these may also have changed over time and not been recorded in the statistics.

ⓔ 3/5 marks awarded.

(ii) Countries use different currencies and these would need to be changed into the same currency for comparison. Again, population size would vary from country to country, so per capita calculations would make the numbers more meaningful. Standard of living is linked to working and leisure time, and countries with different working weeks would have to take them into account when comparing living standards. Around the world, different countries will have different climates and this could affect energy costs.

ⓔ 3/5 marks awarded. This is brief but at least three good points are made.

(e) There are four main ways that government can manage an economy. These are:
- fiscal policy
- monetary policy
- exchange rate policy
- supply-side policy

Using fiscal policy — which changes the balance of expenditure and taxation — the government can budget for a deficit and boost aggregate demand to stimulate economic activity.

Monetary policy is using interest rates and changes in the money supply to stimulate demand and encourage investment. An expansion in the money supply and lower interest rates will make investment in capital more attractive.

Exchange rate policy can have an uncertain effect on economic growth, as lowering exchange rates may boost export sales but at the same time raise the cost of imports.

On the supply side of the economy the government can do things to boost economic growth such as:
- lower taxes to motivate the workforce
- improve education and training
- improve the infrastructure

ⓔ 9/18 marks awarded. The answer is brief and tends to explain rather than discuss points. A discussion involves at least two sides to the argument. Also, although it is reasonably well written, a quality of written communication mark is lost because the continuous prose, which the examiner expects, is punctuated by lists.

ⓔ Scored 37/60　62% = Grade C

Question 2 International trade

Time allowed: I hour 30 minutes

Read the case study below. There are quality of written communication marks in (e) only and it should be answered in continuous prose. Total marks allocated: 60

Table 1 UK balance of payments (£m)

	Balance of trade	Invisible balance	Other balances	Current balance
2004	−48,607	19,162	14,524	−14,921
2005	−60,893	25,918	15,649	−19,326
2006	−68,789	24,611	13,726	−30,452
2007	−83,631	29,194	6,656	−47,781

Table 2 Comparisons between the UK and Japan

	Exchange rate (yen/£)	Consumer price index (2006 = 100)		GDP growth rate (%)	
		UK	Japan	UK	Japan
2004	191	96.7	100.3	2.8	−0.3
2005	187	98.0	100.2	3.3	2.7
2006	198	100	100.0	2.5	2.6
2007	203	102.3	100.2	2.8	2.1

The UK balance of payments showed a marked deterioration on the current balance between 2004 and 2007. Preceding this period the UK had run a tight fiscal policy and a more expansionary monetary policy. During this period both fiscal and monetary policy were expansionary. In comparison, in 2004 Japan was worried about an economic recession and a *lack* of investment, so it reduced its official interest rate to 0.2%.

(a) Explain what is meant by the following economic terms:
(i) balance of trade	(2 marks)
(ii) current balance	(2 marks)
(iii) economic recession	(2 marks)
(iv) investment	(2 marks)

ⓔ Only a brief explanation is required for 2 marks.

(b) (i) The balance of payments will always produce a zero balance. Explain this statement and identify what is missing from the statistics in Table I. (4 marks)

(ii) 'A tight fiscal policy and a more expansionary monetary policy' is quoted above. Explain what is meant by this statement. (4 marks)

(iii) Describe what is meant by a current balance deficit and current balance surplus and say whether it would be possible for a country to be continuously in deficit on its current account. (6 marks)

ⓔ Be guided by the mark allocations as more detail will be required of the macroeconomic targets and policies mentioned in the questions.

(c) (i) **Using only evidence from Tables I and 2, suggest reasons for the changes that have taken place in the value of the yen to the pound between 2004 and 2007.** (6 marks)
   (ii) **What evidence in Table 2 explains why Japan is worried about recession and what effect is lowering interest rates to 0.2% likely to have on the Japanese economy?** (2 marks)
   (iii) **If the rate of interest in Japan was 0.2% in 2004, explain whether the real rate of interest was positive or negative.** (2 marks)

ⓔ Note that it is important to use evidence in the tables to answer these questions.

(d) Explain how the exchange rate of a country is determined and identify the factors that may cause the rate to change. (10 marks)

ⓔ Think of the exchange rate as a price in the market for currency.

(e) Despite the advantages of free trade, almost all countries have protected themselves to a greater or lesser extent from totally free trade. Identify the main trade barriers and discuss whether such protection is a benefit to an economy. (18 marks)

ⓔ Only an explanation of protective trade barriers is required, but a discussion of whether they provide economic benefits completes the answer.

Mark scheme

(a) (i) Must show clear understanding that a balance is the difference between two totals — in this case, goods exported and imported (2 marks).
  (ii) The two totals are goods and services exported and imported (2 marks).
 (iii) A downturn in economic activity that may lead to a depression (2 marks). Alternatively, the student may refer to the more precise measure of two successive quarters of negative economic growth.
 (iv) Needs to refer to the purchase of capital goods (2 marks).

(b) (i) For an explanation of the accounting identity (3 marks). For recognising that the financial account or capital account or balancing item is missing (1 mark); to get this mark it is acceptable to make reference to only one of these items.
  (ii) For an explanation of tight fiscal policy (2 marks) and expansionary monetary policy (2 marks).
 (iii) Descriptions of current balance deficit (2 marks) and current balance surplus (2 marks). An explanation of why it would be difficult for a country to run a persistent deficit in terms of limited foreign exchange reserves and a limited ability to borrow foreign currency (2 marks).

(c) (i) It is necessary to explain that the yen has risen in value between 2004 and 2005 and then fallen in value against the pound from 2005 to 2007. The rise in value could be linked to stable prices in Japan compared with the UK and the UK current balance deficit, while the fall in value could be linked to faster rates of growth in the UK (6 marks).
  (ii) Look for any two of the following: a negative growth rate; the fall in the consumer price index; the rise in the external value of the currency. The lowering of interest rates may be aimed at boosting investment and increasing consumer demand (2 marks).

(iii) The real rate of interest is positive because the rate of inflation is negative and the rate of interest is positive (2 marks).

(d) Allocate approximately half of the marks to an explanation (supported by a diagram) of how an exchange rate is determined in a free market through the interaction of supply and demand. The answer may include a reference to fixed and floating rates. The other half of the marks should be allocated to identifying the factors which shift either the supply curve or the demand curve for currency and produce a new equilibrium rate (10 marks).

(e) Expect a brief mention of the gains from trade that derive from the specialisation of function (2 marks). For identifying the main trade barriers (6 marks) and for discussing the economic advantages and disadvantages of trade barriers (6 marks + 4 marks for quality of written communication).

A-grade answer

(a) **(i)** The balance of trade is the difference between the total value of exported goods and the total value of imported goods over a given period of time. It does not include trade in services.

(e) **2/2 marks awarded.**

(ii) The current balance is the difference between the total value of exported goods and services and the total value of imported goods and services over a given period of time.

(e) **2/2 marks awarded.**

(iii) An economic recession is usually described as a slowdown or downturn in economic activity. This may be characterised by rising unemployment, falling incomes and an increase in bankruptcies.

(e) **2/2 marks awarded.**

(iv) Investment is when a person sets aside some income to buy stocks and shares in order to receive dividends and make a capital gain.

(e) **0/2 marks awarded.** The student makes a common mistake here. Remember that in economics, investment refers to the buying of capital goods like machinery.

(b) **(i)** When people buy imports, they supply their currency to buy foreign currency. When foreigners want to buy UK exports, they supply their currency to buy the exporter's currency. In the UK, if there is not sufficient foreign currency to be bought, then the official reserves have to be run down or foreign currency has to be borrowed. The result of this is that all the unofficial trades in the balance of payments will have to be matched by an official adjustment to currencies that will produce an overall zero balance. In the statistics in Table 1, the capital account and financial account are missing.

ⓔ 4/4 marks awarded.

> **(ii)** Fiscal policy is using the government's budget to manage the overall level of economic activity. A tight fiscal policy occurs when the government reduces expenditure and/or increases taxation in order to reduce aggregate demand. An expansionary monetary policy takes place when the Bank of England reduces interest rates in an attempt to boost aggregate monetary demand.

ⓔ 3/4 marks awarded. In answering this question the student is expected to make reference to increasing the money supply as well as reducing interest rates under an expansionary monetary policy.

> **(iii)** A current balance deficit occurs on the balance of payments when the value of imported goods and services exceeds the value of exported goods and services over a given period of time. This situation is reversed for a current balance surplus when the value of exported goods and services is greater than the corresponding imports.
>
> Many countries, including the UK and the USA, have run current balance deficits for long periods of time, but technically it is not possible to persistently run a deficit because there are limited foreign exchange reserves in a country. Also, a persistent deficit is likely to lead to a fall in the exchange rate and this makes it more difficult to borrow foreign currencies, as foreign countries lose confidence in the country's ability to maintain the value of its currency.

ⓔ 6/6 marks awarded.

> **(c)** **(i)** The value of the pound against the yen fell from 191 yen to 187 yen between 2004 and 2005. This may have been because of the large current account deficit and the higher rate of inflation in the UK. However, between 2005 and 2007, the pound increased in value against the yen from 1 pound buying 187 yen to it buying 203 yen. This could be as a result of the faster rate of economic growth in the UK.

ⓔ 6/6 marks awarded.

> **(ii)** Japan is worried about the likelihood of an economic recession because the consumer price index indicates a deflation, falling from 100.3 to 100, and the GDP was negative in 2004.

ⓔ 2/2 marks awarded. The student has not attempted to explain the effect of lower interest rates on the Japanese economy but still gains full marks.

(iii) In 2004 the consumer price index fell, while the rate of interest was 0.2%. Therefore the real interest rate was made positive by adding the nominal rate of interest to the negative rate of inflation.

(e) **2/2 marks awarded.**

(d) If a currency was floating freely against other currencies, then it would have its value determined on foreign exchange markets by the interaction of supply and demand, as illustrated in the diagram below.

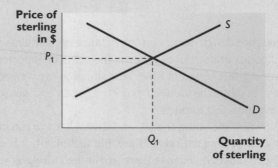

On the vertical axis the price of a currency can only be measured using another currency, hence the value of sterling is being determined by the dollar. The demand for sterling is caused by the demand for UK exports while the supply of sterling is caused by UK demand for imports. P_1Q_1 is the equilibrium exchange rate where the supply of currency meets the demand.

The factors that may cause the exchange rate to change are those that will shift the demand and supply curve for currency. For example, foreigners may demand more of our exports if they become relatively cheaper or are of improved quality or as a result of a change in tastes and preferences in other countries. All of these will shift the demand curve to the right and raise the equilibrium exchange rate.

In a similar way, if these things happen in the domestic economy then the increase in the demand for imports will shift the supply curve to the right and produce an equilibrium at a lower exchange rate.

(e) **8/10 marks awarded.** This is a good answer which deals equally well with both parts of the question.

(e) If all countries traded freely, then firms within these countries would be able to gain from trade by specialising in those products for which they had a comparative advantage, i.e. they would produce more of those products in which they have a lower opportunity cost of production.

There are many ways that a country can choose to protect itself against imports. The most commonly used trade barrier is to impose a tariff on all or selected imports. The tariff is like a tax and it can be a specific amount or an *ad valorem* tariff. The revenue collected goes to the Treasury.

A second fairly common method of protection is to impose a quota on a foreign country or a foreign product. This limits the quantity that can be imported over a specific period of time and can often benefit firms which have a share of the quota, as the restricted supply allows them to raise prices and increase profit margins.

A variety of domestic policies can be used to protect domestic industry and disadvantage potential competition from abroad. A government may choose to subsidise domestic industry and this will allow it to undercut the price of imports. It is possible to use legislation to protect domestic industry. In Tokyo, only Japanese-made cars were allowed to use the public car parks, which made people think twice about buying a foreign car. It is also possible to use differential tax rates to disadvantage imports. The small Japanese car is a few centimetres narrower than its European competitors, which are then taxed at a higher rate because they are larger cars.

Finally, it is also possible to appeal to the patriotic nature of a country and discourage imports. French farmers have been particularly effective in discouraging farm products from the UK, while the UK has, in the past, used 'Buy British' campaigns to encourage consumers to buy British products.

@ **11/18 marks awarded.** The answer is well written, but the student has not fully addressed the question. The main trade barriers have been identified, but there is little discussion of what benefits these have for the economy, e.g.:
- to protect infant industry
- to protect against illegal imports
- to allow senile industry to regenerate
- national security
- to counter unfair trading practices
- to preserve UK jobs

Scored 48/60   80% = Grade A

C-grade answer

(a) (i) The balance of trade is a measure of all the imports and exports of a country.

@ **0/2 marks awarded.** The student does not identify what is meant by a balance or explain that it is in goods only.

(ii) The current balance measures the state of the balance of payments, including all capital transactions.

@ **0/2 marks awarded.** This answer should not include capital transactions.

(iii) An economic recession means that output is falling, unemployment is rising and incomes are falling. It often comes before a depression and after a boom.

ⓔ **2/2 marks awarded.**

(iv) Investment takes place when current consumption is foregone and resources are allocated to the production of factories and machines.

ⓔ **2/2 marks awarded.**

(b) **(i)** The balance of payments will always produce a zero balance. This is because the value of everything leaving the country in the form of exports must be equal to the value of everything entering the country. Any shortfall of foreign currency will be made up from the government's foreign exchange reserves. There is something missing from Table 1 because the numbers in each year do not add up to zero.

ⓔ **2/4 marks awarded.** The student does not know what is missing from Table 1. The first part of the answer is not particularly well explained, although it does show some understanding.

(ii) Taxation is a withdrawal from the circular flow of income while expenditure is an injection. Fiscal policy is using the budget to change the overall level of aggregate demand in the economy. If more money is withdrawn from the economy by taxation than is injected into the economy, then it would be described as a tight fiscal policy. An expansionary monetary policy is one that would allow the money supply to expand and interest rates to fall. This would expand aggregate monetary demand in the economy.

ⓔ **4/4 marks awarded.**

(iii) A current balance deficit is when the balance of payments shows a deficit before any official financing, whereas a surplus does not require official financing. It would not be possible for a country to run a current balance deficit continually, as it has neither sufficient reserves of foreign currency to fill the gap, nor unlimited capacity to borrow from other countries.

ⓔ **2/6 marks awarded.** The student doesn't understand what is meant by a current balance surplus or deficit, but is awarded marks for commenting on whether a deficit can be continuously run.

(c) **(i)** The value of the yen rose against the pound between 2004 and 2005 from 191 yen being required to buy 1 pound to only 187 yen needed to buy the same pound. The rise could have been the result of the poor performance of the UK external account and the mild deflation in Japan, or due to the slower rates of growth in Japan. This situation could have been reversed between 2005 and 2007, when the value of the yen fell. However, other factors not identifiable from the table could also be important, e.g. different rates of interest.

@ **6/6 marks awarded.**

> **(ii)** The Japanese are worried about a recession because the growth rate of GDP
> has become negative (−0.3% in 2004). Lowering interest rates may encourage
> investment and help to increase the growth rate.

@ **2/2 marks awarded.** The student misses evidence from the consumer prices index and the
effect of a lower interest rate on consumer spending but still gains full marks.

> **(iii)** The real rate of interest is a positive number, i.e. 0.2%.

@ **0/2 marks awarded.** The student does not understand what is meant by 'real'.

(d) The exchange rate of a country is determined by the supply of currency to the
foreign exchange market and the demand from the same market. Supply of
currency is determined by the demand for imports, while the demand for currency
is determined by the demand for exports. In the diagram below, the price of a
currency is measured by another currency, and the intersection of the supply and
demand curve is the equilibrium exchange rate.

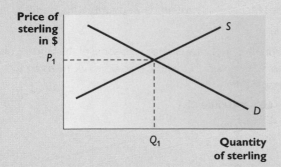

The factors that may cause the exchange rate to change are those that will shift
either the supply curve or the demand curve for currency. The demand curve of
currency to buy exports and the supply curve of currency to buy imports may shift
as the result of:
- a change in taste for UK products abroad and foreign products at home
- different inflation rates between countries
- different rates of economic growth
- different interest rates between countries

@ **6/10 marks awarded.** The first part of the answer is well written. The second part of
the answer includes a list which is not developed, and this cannot be used as a substitute for an
explanation in continuous prose. The points made are relevant and score some marks.

(e) Free trade does produce gains from trade when firms specialise in the product for which they have comparative advantage. However, those gains from trade are not allocated equally and neither may the trade be fair and competitive. For example, a state-run firm in one country, which is heavily subsidised, may have over-produced a product and in order to get rid of the surplus, it may dump them in other countries. This means that they are sold below the true cost of production and they have the potential to force firms out of business in the country where the products are dumped.

In the less developed world, there are many firms which are just starting up and cannot compete with long-established firms in the more developed world. This means that there is an economic argument for protecting those industries against competition for a period of time, until they have expanded production and reduced costs enough to be able to compete with low cash flows. This same argument is used to argue that old and nearly obsolete industry should be protected while it regenerates and shifts its cost curve downwards.

In a world where some countries, like Colombia, produce and export drugs that can be described as demerit goods, other countries may need to protect themselves against their imports by making it illegal to bring them into the country.

There are also other arguments that are not so easy to justify in economic terms, and these include job protection and protecting national security.

ⓔ **10/18 marks awarded.** The answer deals with some of the benefits of protected trade, but it does not identify the main barriers to trade. It is, however, well written and achieves 4 marks for quality of written communication.

ⓔ **Scored 36/60   60% = Grade C**

Question 3 **Changing attitudes to macroeconomic management**

Time allowed: I hour 30 minutes

Read the case study below. There are quality of written communication marks in (e) only and it should be written in continuous prose.

Total marks allocated: 60

Over the last 50 years, there has been considerable discussion over whether the economy can be fine-tuned by manipulating aggregate demand to achieve full employment and stable prices. Fiscal policy has been the main tool of macroeconomic management with an accommodating monetary policy. Critics of this view of macroeconomic management have suggested that there are too many unknown and unpredictable reactions in the economy to the rather blunt tool of demand-side management. These economists have tended to suggest that on the demand side of the economy the best we can hope for is a steady expansion in aggregate demand roughly in line with the growth in output of the economy. If this is the situation, then how do we deal with problems such as slow, sluggish and even negative economic growth? Is there a solution to the problem identified in Figure 1 below?

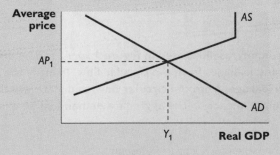

Figure 1

Here, the current equilibrium situation for the economy is at Y_1AP_1. The economy has a relatively high level of unemployment and is not achieving its full productive potential which is to the right of Y_1. An alternative view put forward by other economists is that the government should adopt and promote supply-side policies that will shift the supply curve outward to achieve equilibrium at a higher level of economic activity.

(a) Briefly answer the following questions:
   (i) What is meant by an economy's productive potential?   (2 marks)
   (ii) What is the difference between an aggregate supply curve and an aggregate demand curve?   (2 marks)

🌐 Highlight the difference between the two curves, do not just explain each curve.

(iii) Distinguish between monetary and fiscal policy. (3 marks)

ⓔ Say what is different about the two policies.

(iv) What is meant by the statement 'fiscal policy has been the main tool of macroeconomic management with an accommodating monetary policy'? (3 marks)

(b) (i) Identify the four main components of aggregate demand. (4 marks)

ⓔ Just knowledge recall is required here.

(ii) Explain why the aggregate demand curve in Figure 1 is downward sloping from left to right. (4 marks)

(iii) Explain what is meant by a person's disposable income and their marginal propensity to consume. (2 marks)

(iv) With reference to the 'marginal propensity to consume', explain how it may cause a shift in the aggregate demand curve. (3 marks)

ⓔ Focus on a shift and do not describe a movement as the initial change.

(c) (i) Explain, with the use of a diagram, an outward shift in an aggregate supply curve and offer two reasons that explain why the curve may have shifted to the right. (6 marks)

ⓔ Your answer must include a diagram to access full marks.

(ii) The equilibrium position for the economy, as illustrated in Figure 1 by Y_1, can be disturbed by injections into the circular flow and leakages from the circular flow. Identify the three main injections and the three main leakages from the circular flow, and state whether it is more likely that they will have an initial impact on the aggregate demand curve or the aggregate supply curve. (4 marks)

ⓔ Refer to the diagram when answering this question.

(d) (i) How is unemployment measured? (3 marks)

(ii) What are the arguments for using either demand management or supply-side policies to reduce the problem of unused productive potential? (6 marks)

ⓔ This is not a discussion — it is just asking for supporting explanation.

(e) What is sustainable economic growth? Discuss the costs and benefits of achieving a high rate of economic growth. (18 marks)

ⓔ The first part requires an explanation, but the second part requires an evaluation of good and bad effects.

Mark scheme

(a) (i) Explain the full use of an economy's productive factors. The answer may include a production possibility boundary (2 marks).

(ii) An explanation of the upward-sloping supply curve (1 mark) and the downward-sloping demand curve (1 mark).

(iii) Monetary policy (1 mark), fiscal policy (1 mark) and a distinguishing comment (1 mark).

(iv) An explanation in terms of how the government has used the difference between taxation and expenditure to manage the economy and the possible effect it could have on monetary policy (3 marks).

(b) (i) Consumer expenditure (1 mark), government expenditure (1 mark), investment (1 mark), the balance between exports and imports (1 mark).

(ii) An explanation may include the increased foreign demand for exports at lower prices, the real income effect of falling prices, the wealth effect of falling prices, and the expectations of rises in the future (4 marks). At least two of the above explained well can gain maximum marks.

(iii) Explain disposable income (1 mark), and marginal propensity to consume (1 mark).

(iv) Explain a shift and say how an increase or decrease in the marginal propensity to consume can change consumer expenditure, which is the main component of aggregate demand (3 marks).

(c) (i) An explanation of any two of the following: (4 marks)
- increased investment and business
- increased technical efficiency, invention and innovation
- improved training and education
- increased incentive to work and work harder
- improvements in geographical and occupational mobility

Plus a labelled diagram to illustrate (2 marks).

(ii) Savings and investment (1 mark), taxation and government expenditure (1 mark), imports and exports (1 mark), likely to affect aggregate demand (1 mark).

(d) (i) Common measures include those who register for unemployment benefits and the sample 'Labour Force Survey'. Other measures may be included (3 marks).

(ii) It will be necessary to explain how fiscal, monetary and exchange rate policies can be used to manipulate aggregate demand, including some assessment of their likely efficacy; or the impact of supply-side policies, including the likelihood of their success (6 marks).

(e) The student must identify sustainability as well as offer some evaluation of either the likely costs or benefits of a high rate of economic growth, which may or may not be considered sustainable (14 marks + 4 marks for quality of written communication).

A-grade answer

(a)   (i) At any one point in time, an economy has a finite capacity to produce goods and services given its factors of production. This is called its productive potential and can be illustrated by a production possibility boundary. If a country has unemployed resources, then it is producing below its productive potential.

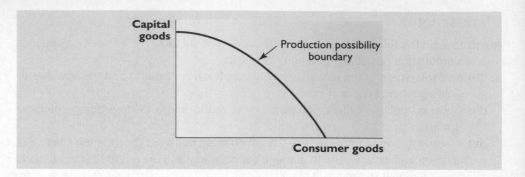

ⓔ **2/2 marks awarded.**

(ii) An aggregate supply curve illustrates the functional relationship between the real GDP and the average level of prices. It is upward sloping, meaning that at higher average prices more output is produced. In contrast, the aggregate demand curve is downward sloping, meaning that at lower average prices more will be demanded.

ⓔ **2/2 marks awarded.**

(iii) Monetary policy is when the Bank of England uses interest rates and its controls over the money supply to manage the overall level of monetary demand. In contrast, the Treasury is concerned with overseeing fiscal policy, which is using the budget to change the overall balance between taxation and expenditure and therefore the overall level of aggregate demand.

ⓔ **3/3 marks awarded.**

(iv) The statement means that the government has been mainly concerned with managing the demand side of the economy using budget deficits to expand the economy and surpluses to dampen down demand. These policies tend to have a secondary effect on monetary policy, e.g. a budget deficit could cause interest rates to rise to finance the borrowing requirement.

ⓔ **3/3 marks awarded.** Top marks for part (a).

(b) (i) The main components of aggregate demand are consumer expenditure, government expenditure and investment expenditure.

ⓔ **3/4 marks awarded.** The student missed out exports–imports.

(ii) The aggregate demand curve is downward sloping from left to right because — as the average level of prices falls — more foreigners are attracted to buy UK products. People in the UK would find an increase in their real income at lower prices, and also a substitution effect as UK consumers find domestic products cheaper to buy than the competing imported product.

e **4/4 marks awarded.**

(iii) Disposable income is what is left over to spend after a person's total income is reduced by claims in the form of taxation, national insurance and pensions. The marginal propensity to consume (MPC) is how much of an additional pound received a consumer will spend. If it is 80p then MPC = 80p/100p = 0.8.

e **2/2 marks awarded.**

(iv) If we assume that the marginal propensity to consume is 0.8 and something happens to reduce it to 0.7, then this will reduce consumer expenditure. As consumer expenditure is the main component of aggregate demand, so the aggregate demand curve shifts to the left. The reverse happens if the MPC increases.

e **3/3 marks awarded.**

(c)   (i)

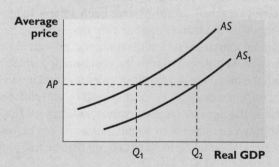

An outward shift in the aggregate supply curve means that more output is being supplied at each and every average price. This may be caused by increases in investment, or the invention of new products.

e **4/6 marks awarded.** The diagram scores 2 marks, but the two reasons are stated rather than explained. Therefore the student loses 2 marks.

(ii) Consumer expenditure, government expenditure, investment, savings, taxation and imports. Changes in any of these will affect the aggregate demand curve.

e **2/4 marks awarded.** Consumer expenditure is not an injection, and mention of exports is missed out.

(d) (i) The level of unemployment in the economy is recorded by adding together all those people who register as unemployed and therefore claim benefits. This means that unemployment is probably understated, because people who do not claim these benefits are not included in the statistics. Also, surveys are carried out in selected proportions of the population, from which estimates of unemployment can be made.

ⓔ **3/3 marks awarded.**

(ii)

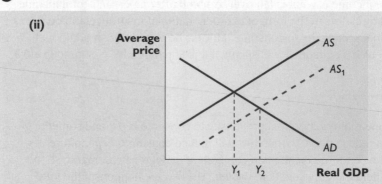

In the diagram above, Y_1 represents the current equilibrium position for an economy with unused productive potential. Y_2 represents the position where all resources are fully employed. To reach this point using supply-side policies, the AS curve will need to shift its position to AS_1.

Over recent years there seems to have been a move to using supply-side policies to motivate the worker and the firm into working harder. This may involve lowering marginal rates of taxation or corporation tax. It could be done through education and training programmes which are aimed at improving the quality of productive factors and making the UK more competitive on world markets. If successful, they will shift the aggregate supply curve to the right. Some economists have argued that it may be a good idea to encourage an increase in output, but it will not be very effective if there is not the additional demand to take up these extra products.

ⓔ **5/6 marks awarded.** This is a good attempt at explaining how unemployment is measured (part i) and discussing the likely effectiveness of supply-side policies (part ii).

(e) Economic growth is when there is an increase in the per capita productive capacity of an economy. It is illustrated by an outward shift in the economy's production possibility boundary.

Economic growth can result from activities that are both sustainable and unsustainable. For example, a slash and burn approach to farming in equatorial areas will increase economic growth, but at the same time it will destroy hardwood forest that will take hundreds of years to replace, as well as making the soil unusable after a few years of farming. Sustainable economic growth should allow the economy to grow but not reduce the availability of resources to future generations.

A high rate of economic growth will produce benefits to society. It will increase the availability of goods and services to all people and this will fulfil the aspirations of people who want to become better off, and it will do it in a way that does not take things away from other people. Also it will allow government to pursue policies that require increased expenditure and it will not require increased taxation rates to finance it. Alternatively, the tax burden could be reduced without having to cut public expenditure.

However, economic growth and, even more so, faster rates of economic growth, impose costs on society. The first cost is the opportunity cost of allocating resources to capital investment, which produces a reduction in current consumption such that standards of living in the present will be reduced in order to increase them in the future.

There are also personal costs to individuals, as faster rates of economic growth require people to take on new jobs. As skills become redundant, people will have to retrain and perhaps suffer periods of unemployment. These things impose stress upon people, especially as they are likely to be made redundant and be asked to take on a new job at a time in their life when they are less able to cope.

A final area of costs to society is the external costs of production and consumption as the economy grows. Increased production raises the risk of pollution, although it can be argued that economic growth produces the opportunity to clean up pollution or search for cleaner, greener ways to produce things. On the side of consumption, people's increased income will often lead to the purchase of more cars and this will increase exhaust pollution and congestion on our roads. Both of these impose considerable costs on society, which government has recently tried to tackle by imposing taxes on petrol carbon emissions and large vehicles with inefficient engines.

Overall, economic growth is not all good news and economists need to weigh carefully the costs and benefits to society to ensure that growth is sustainable and does not just give today's generation a quick fix at the expense of damaging the society in which future generations will have to live.

@ **15/18 marks awarded.** This is a good answer which attempts a sound discussion of the issues surrounding economic growth and also achieves the maximum 4 marks for the quality of its written communication.

@ **Scored 51/60   85% = Grade A**

C-grade answer

(a) **(i)** Theoretically this is the total amount of products that can be produced by one country at one point in time. If a country has unemployed resources, then it is producing below its productive potential.

ⓔ **2/2 marks awarded.**

(ii) An aggregate supply curve shows the total amount that can be produced in an economy and an aggregate demand curve shows the total amount that is being consumed at various prices.

ⓔ **1/2 marks awarded.** This is a brief statement about what is meant by aggregate supply and demand, with just a hint at the functional relationship between price and output.

(iii) Fiscal policy is how the government uses its budget. Monetary policy is how the government uses interest rates and money supply.

ⓔ **2/3 marks awarded.** The student loses a mark because the answer is not fully explained.

(iv) This statement means that governments use the budget as a main tool of economic management most of the time and only use monetary policy occasionally.

ⓔ **0/3 marks awarded.** The student misses the point that it is the relationship between fiscal and monetary policy which is being questioned.

(b) **(i)** They are consumer expenditure, investment, government expenditure and net expenditure on imports and exports.

ⓔ **4/4 marks awarded.**

(ii) Aggregate demand curves are downward sloping from left to right because as product prices fall, so people can afford to buy more. This, of course, assumes that their income does not fall as well.

ⓔ **1/4 marks awarded.** The student needs to develop the answer more fully (see A-grade answer).

(iii) Disposable income is what is left in your pay after taxes and other things have been removed. The marginal propensity to consume is the proportion of each additional pound earned that you spend.

ⓔ **2/2 marks awarded.**

> **(iv)** If everyone's marginal propensity to consume goes up, then the aggregate demand curve shifts outwards, whereas it shifts inwards if their MPC goes down.

ⓔ **2/3 marks awarded.** This answer is fine, but a fuller explanation is required for 3/3 marks.

(c) (i)

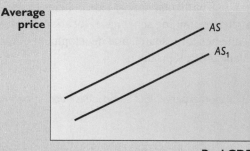

> An outward shift in the supply curve from *AS* to *AS₁* is an increase in the output of the economy which is not caused by a change in price. Economic growth in terms of an increase in the productive potential of an economy could have accounted for this.

ⓔ **2/6 marks awarded.** The student seems to have dried up after writing about economic growth. An explanation of the various causes of economic growth — e.g. investment, invention and innovation — could have improved the mark.

> **(ii)** The main injections into the circular flow are government expenditure, investment and exports. These are matched by the following leakages — taxation, saving and imports. If any of these change, they are likely to affect the aggregate demand curve first.

ⓔ **4/4 marks awarded.**

> **(d) (i)** There are two main measures of unemployment. They are the Claimant Count, which adds up all those people claiming unemployment benefits, and the Labour Force Survey, which is an estimate taken from a sample survey of all those people who are without jobs, but who are available to work and are seeking employment. This is generally a larger number than the Claimant Count, but it is subject to the errors associated with sampling.

ⓔ **3/3 marks awarded.**

(ii) It is argued that a significant amount of unemployment is due to deficient aggregate demand and that the government can boost aggregate monetary demand by using fiscal and/or monetary policy. Using fiscal policy, the government can budget for a deficit, which means it spends more money than it takes in taxation. Alternatively, or in addition to fiscal policy, the Bank of England can pursue an expansionary policy by lowering rates of interest and encouraging an expansion of credit. For other forms of unemployment, the government can use particular supply-side policies to boost employment. These could include retraining schemes, relocation schemes, motivational schemes and schemes for research and development to increase the quality and competitiveness of UK products.

4/6 marks awarded. Good in part (i) but some ideas need to be more fully developed in part (ii).

(e) Economic growth is an increase in the productive capacity per person in an economy. When this occurs, it shifts the production possibility frontier outwards. For economic growth to be sustainable, non-renewable resources have to be replaced and/or recycled in the production process.

It is usual for people to expect that over their working life they will become better off and each successive generation hopes that it will be richer than the last. Governments also want to be able to do more to help the citizens of their country. All of these things can be achieved when an economy is growing.

However, growth can cause problems. There is an opportunity cost of investment, which is a reduction in current consumption. There is a personal cost, as a growing economy requires things to change and the workforce to be mobile. There are many frictions in the labour force that restrict occupational and geographical mobility.

Finally, growth carries external costs to society, such as pollution and congestion. Also, economic growth can lead to resources being used up more quickly and this may go against sustainability.

10/18 marks awarded. Some good points are made, but generally this answer is too brief and lacking in evaluative comment. It may be that this student's time management was at fault and not enough time was set aside to complete this last question, which is a shame. It is, however, well written and scores the maximum 4 marks for the quality of written communication.

Scored 37/60   62% = Grade C

Question 4 The euro: a good idea?

Time allowed: 1 hour 30 minutes

Read the case study below. There are quality of written communication marks in (e) only and it should be answered in continuous prose.

Total marks allocated: 60

Table 1 European interest, growth and inflation rates

	Interest rates (%)	Growth rates (%)	Inflation rates (%)
1998			
UK	7.4	2.6	2.3
France	3.6	3.2	0.6
Germany	3.5	1.8	0.9
Italy	4.8	1.5	2.0
Ireland	5.6	8.9	2.4
1999			
UK	5.4	2.1	2.1
France	2.9	2.9	0.5
Germany	2.9	1.4	0.6
Italy	2.9	1.4	1.7
Ireland	2.9	8.0	1.6

At the beginning of 1999, some members of the EU — including France, Germany, Italy and Ireland — irrevocably fixed their currencies to the euro and agreed a date for the replacement of their domestic currencies by the euro. The UK postponed joining the single European currency and, since that time, the value of the pound sterling has varied significantly against the euro. One of the main advantages of joining a single currency is a reduction in the costs of trading in many currencies and an increase in trade between those countries which are using the single unit of account. The main concern of the UK was the need for interest rates to converge, alongside the loss of control over monetary policy and exchange rate policy, plus the severe limits that would be imposed on the budget and fiscal policy.

(a) (i) What are the UK and Eurozone measures for inflation?   (2 marks)
    (ii) What was the real rate of interest in each country in 1998?   (2 marks)
    (iii) Use production possibility curves to illustrate the difference between growth in output and economic growth.   (3 marks)
    (iv) Explain what is meant when the pound sterling appreciates against the euro.   (1 mark)

ⓔ Only brief answers are required here, but make sure you use diagrams in part (iii).

(b) (i) **Explain and illustrate how interest rates are determined in a free market.** (4 marks)

(ii) **Explain how interest rates are determined in the UK and the Eurozone.** (4 marks)

(iii) **Looking at the interest rates for 1998 and 1999, explain why the UK may have been reluctant to join the euro in 1999.** (4 marks)

ⓔ 'Illustrate' means that you must include a diagram to get full marks in part (i); part (ii) is best answered with a diagram; and part (iii) requires a reasoned explanation — it does not have to be factually correct.

(c) (i) **Using the figures in Table 1, suggest whether the UK was right to think that joining the euro would raise its inflation rate and lower its growth rate.** (4 marks)

(ii) **Explain what is meant by the UK being concerned about 'the loss of control over monetary policy and exchange rate policy'.** (4 marks)

(iii) **Explain what is meant by the 'severe limits that would be imposed on the budget and fiscal policy'.** (4 marks)

ⓔ Part (i) requires you to interpret the figures in Table 1, while the other two parts require you to look at the main macroeconomic policies in a Eurozone context.

(d) **What are the effects on an economy of high accelerating inflation as opposed to low stable inflation?** (10 marks)

ⓔ Look at the damaging effects of high and accelerating inflation as opposed to the relative benefits of low and stable inflation.

(e) **What is meant by the conflicts that occur in pursuit of the main macroeconomic policy objectives of government? Discuss whether fiscal and monetary policy can be used independently of each other to manage the economy.** (18 marks)

ⓔ Explain the conflicts, but look for an argument to develop in the second part of the question.

Mark scheme

(a) (i) UK = consumer price index (CPI) (1 mark), Eurozone is the harmonised index of consumer prices (HICP) (1 mark).

(ii) Interest rate – inflation = real rate of interest, therefore UK = 5.1; France = 3.0; Germany = 2.6; Italy = 2.8; and Ireland = 3.2 (2 marks if all are correct, 1 mark if one or more are incorrect).

(iii) Diagram correctly labelled (1 mark), an explanation of a movement from inside the boundary towards the boundary (1 mark), shifting the boundary outwards (1 mark).

(iv) On foreign exchange markets, fewer pounds will be required to buy the same quantity of euros (1 mark).

(b) (i) Diagram correctly labelled (1 mark), explanation of demand for money and supply of money (3 marks). If a student uses loanable funds rather than liquidity preference theory, then allocate full marks.

(ii) Bank of England intervention in the UK (2 marks), European Central Bank (ECB) in Europe (2 marks).

(iii) Expect a recognition of relatively high rates in the UK compared with other countries and the low target set by the ECB (4 marks).

(c) (i) Growth rates and inflation rates both fell in the UK as they did for all the other countries, therefore there is no evidence to support the UK concern (4 marks).

(ii) Joining the euro fixes the pound against the euro and leaves the ECB to determine the rate with the rest of the world. Also, interest rates of 2.9% could be imposed on the UK (4 marks).

(iii) Given exchange rate and interest rate targets are set externally, the UK will have to be careful about the balance between taxation and expenditure, particularly in the case of a budget deficit (4 marks).

(d) Expect a clear explanation of what is meant by 'high accelerating inflation' and 'low stable inflation', and some of the following:
- loss of purchasing power
- loss of confidence in the use of money
- indiscriminate redistributions of income and wealth
- loss of business confidence
- shoe leather and menu costs
- damaging effect on the exchange rate and interest rates

The student may see more advantages of low and stable inflation because this:
- avoids deflation
- stimulates the economy
- avoids falling nominal wages
- creates predictable borrowing rates and repayments
  (10 marks)

(e) Explain how policies aimed at achieving any individual target set out below could aggravate the other targets of:
- low inflation
- high employment
- balance of payments equilibrium
- faster economic growth

Expect some discussion of the effects that an expansionary fiscal policy can have on the money supply and interest rates, and how a contractionary monetary policy may impose a limit on the way in which a public sector borrowing requirement can be financed (14 marks + 4 marks for quality of written communication).

A-grade answer

(a) (i) The consumer price index is used to measure inflation in the UK, while the harmonised index of consumer prices is used to measure inflation in Eurozone countries.

🄔 **2/2 marks awarded.**

(ii) In 1998, the real rate of interest in each country is the nominal rate minus the rate of inflation:

UK = 5.1%	✓
France = 3.0%	✓
Germany = 2.4%	✗
Italy = 2.8%	✓
Ireland = 3.2%	✓

🄔 **1/2 marks awarded.** The student made a careless mistake with the German rate.

(iii)

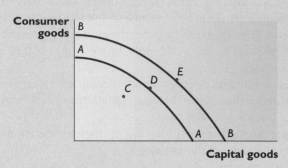

Economic growth is when the productive capacity of an economy increases. This shifts the boundary *AA–BB*. Therefore *D–E* is economic growth. If there are unemployed resources, then the economy can expand output from inside the boundary as illustrated by a move from *C* to *D*.

ⓔ **3/3 marks awarded.**

(iv) The pound sterling appreciates in a floating exchange rate system when the price of sterling rises against the foreign currency. It means that the same pound will now buy more foreign currency.

ⓔ **1/1 mark awarded.**

(b) (i)

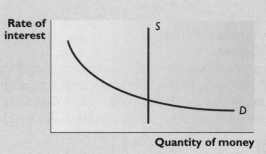

The supply of money is perfectly inelastic as it is exogenously determined by the Bank of England. The demand for money, which is given its shape by the speculative demand but also includes transactions and precautionary demand, is downward sloping from left to right. Where the two curves intersect is the equilibrium rate of interest.

ⓔ **4/4 marks awarded.**

(ii) In the UK and the Eurozone, interest rates are not free to be determined by market forces, but the Bank of England and the European Central Bank intervene in the markets to set rates. They do this through the buying and selling of short-term government securities that maintain the required liquidity in the banking system and fix the agreed rate.

(e) **4/4 marks awarded.**

(iii) In 1998, the interest rate in the UK was 7.4%, while the average for the four Eurozone countries was 4.4%. In 1999, the UK rate was 5.4% and the Eurozone rate was 2.9%. It would therefore be the case that if the UK wanted to join the euro, it would have had to lower its interest rate to such an extent that many variables in the economy, like borrowing, savings and investment, would have been considerably disturbed.

(e) **4/4 marks awarded.**

(c) **(i)** Between 1998 and 1999 the growth rate in the UK fell from 2.6% to 2.1%, which is a fall of 19.2%, while the average rate for the other countries fell by only 10.9%. Also, the inflation rate fell from 2.3% to 2.1%, which is a fall of 8.7%, while the average for the other countries was a fall of 25.4%. Without reference to any other evidence, it would seem that the UK was wrong, because its growth rates were lower than the other countries and inflation rates were higher and fell less.

(e) **4/4 marks awarded.**

(ii) If the UK joined the euro, then the ECB would gain control over UK monetary policy and exchange rate policy.

(e) **1/4 marks awarded.** There is only one relevant point in this answer and it is a brief statement rather than an explanation.

(iii) The UK would not be able to do anything in its budget or in pursuit of fiscal control over the economy that would affect the monetary targets, which are established by the European Central Bank.

(e) **3/4 marks awarded.** The student should have given more detail in the explanation.

(d) A high accelerating rate of inflation would mean that the monthly rates would be rising and could reach what is termed hyperinflation, where prices rise by hundreds and thousands of percent per month. This type of inflation tends to damage the economy, although a few people, such as those who own lots of real assets, may not be affected. Alternatively, a low and stable rate of inflation may have more benefits than costs to an economy.

A high rate of inflation brings about an indiscriminate redistribution of income and wealth. Those on fixed incomes become worse off while those who hold their assets in the form of money may see its value wiped out.

There are shoe leather costs of inflation, as people hold minimum active money balances and are forever running to and from the bank. Also, there are menu costs of inflation, as prices have to be changed regularly at the restaurant and petrol pump. Another damaging effect of high inflation is the loss of business confidence that results from unstable prices, falling exchange rates and rising interest rates.

In contrast to the damage done by high rates of inflation, the existence of a low rate of inflation can be a positive benefit to an economy. It can stimulate demand in the economy and make business more buoyant. Business confidence is not damaged, as interest rates and exchange rates will remain fairly stable.

Overall, although all types of inflation bring benefits to some and costs to others, there is probably a net benefit of a low and stable rate of inflation and a net cost to society of high accelerating inflation.

☻ **8/10 marks awarded.** This is a good analysis of the effects.

(e) There are four main macroeconomic policies of government, and these include maintaining a low and stable rate of inflation, a high level of employment, a balance of payments equilibrium and a sustainable rate of economic growth. Using demand management policies, it is difficult to satisfy all of these targets. For example, if the economy has a high level of unemployment, an expansionary fiscal policy may improve levels of employment and may stimulate economic growth, but there is a risk to inflation and the increase in demand for imports may pose a threat to the current account of the balance of payments. Alternatively, a deflationary fiscal policy may help bring down a higher than expected rate of inflation and may improve the current account of the balance of payments, but at the same time may pose threats to the level of employment and the rate of economic growth.

In contrast, supply-side policies may not produce the same conflicts, and policies to promote economic growth through research and development and incentives could benefit both inflation and levels of employment without putting the balance of payments at risk.

Fiscal and monetary policies are often used independently and given a ceteris paribus assumption in theory, whereas in reality they are linked. Under the Keynesian demand management policy, monetary policy was expected to accommodate the proposed changes in fiscal policy as the taxation and expenditure regime of government was the dominant policy. More recently, monetary policy has been the priority and it has imposed a discipline on the extent to which government can run an unbalanced budget.

Let us look at definite links between the two policies. Suppose the government chose to expand the economy by running a budget deficit. In this situation, the deficit will need to be financed. If all the debt can be sold at current rates of interest, then there will be little effect on monetary policy. If, however, all the debt cannot be sold, then the money supply may expand as cash is printed against unsold debt or the rate of interest may be raised to sell the extra debt. In this case, an expansionary fiscal policy may have produced a contractionary monetary policy.

In the current situation (2008), the government is faced with a large budget deficit and a rising level of inflation. If it chooses to raise interest rates to control the rate of inflation, then these higher rates will make it easier to sell additional debt, but at the same time it will increase the level of government expenditure required to service that debt.

Overall, it is both likely that conflicts will exist in the pursuit of macroeconomic goals and that changes in fiscal or monetary policy will have an effect on the other policy.

ⓔ **15/18 marks awarded.** This is a well-written answer with a number of good discussion points. It receives full marks for the quality of written communication.

ⓔ **Scored 50/60   83% = Grade A**

C-grade answer

(a) (i) RPI stands for the retail price index, which is a weighted average index number that represents price changes in the economy, and is used to measure inflation in the UK. A similar index is used in Europe.

ⓔ **1/2 marks awarded.** 1 mark for being historically correct for the UK.

(ii) UK = 5.1%; France = 3.0%; Germany = 2.6%; Italy = 2.8%; Ireland = 3.2%.

ⓔ **1/2 marks awarded.** The student gets the right answer, but does not state what is meant by the real rate of interest and therefore loses 1 mark.

(iii) Growth in an economy can occur when unemployed resources are used and the economy moves closer to its full productive potential.

ⓔ **1/3 marks awarded.** This is a good explanation of growth in output, but it loses 2 marks for not including a diagram and an explanation of economic growth.

(iv) If the pound sterling has appreciated, this means that more pounds will have to be used to buy the same amount of foreign currency.

ⓔ **0/1 mark awarded.** This answer is the wrong way round — the student describes depreciation.

(b) **(i)** In a free market the rate of interest is said to be determined either by the interaction of the supply and demand for money or by the interaction of the supply of savings and the demand for loans.

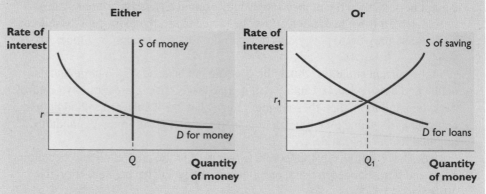

As the rate of interest falls, so the speculative demand for money rises and the demand for loans increases. Meanwhile, the supply of savings falls and the supply of money remains unchanged.

ⓔ **4/4 marks awarded.**

(ii) In the UK and Eurozone, interest rates are determined by market forces but with some government intervention on either the demand or supply side to establish a rate that is consistent with the policy of the UK government or the European Union. In 1999, the UK rate is higher than the Eurozone rate, as illustrated by the figures, i.e. 5.4% and 2.9%.

ⓔ **4/4 marks awarded.**

(iii) Interest rates in the UK are much higher than those in the other countries of Europe.

ⓔ **1/4 marks awarded.** The statement is correct, but there is no explanation of the point.

(c) **(i)** Looking at the statistics in Table 1, there is no evidence that the rate of inflation has increased in any of the countries that are part of the euro. The growth rate, however, has fallen in all the Eurozone countries, but the fact that it has fallen even more in the UK does not suggest that belonging to the euro was the problem.

ⓔ **3/4 marks awarded.** Although this answer is correct, the student needs to make a more precise reference to the statistics in Table 1.

(ii) If the UK joined the single European currency, the European Bank would determine the level of interest rates as well as influencing the exchange rate of the euro against the rest of the world's currencies. Also, there would be no exchange rate between Eurozone countries, therefore it would not be possible to adjust the pound against the franc or the mark.

ⓔ **4/4 marks awarded.**

(iii) Not being able to change interest rates will limit the opportunity to stimulate aggregate demand.

ⓔ **2/4 marks awarded.** This answer is correct as far as it goes, but is not relevant to answering the question.

(d) All rates of inflation have redistributive effects and, with accelerating inflation, these effects are more obvious and potentially more damaging. Inflation reduces the value of money and anyone holding assets in cash will find its value declining. Alternatively, those people holding real assets such as houses are likely to find the value of their assets rising at least nominally if not in real terms.

　　Those people with debts will find the real value of the debts falling, while people with savings will also find their value declining. People on fixed incomes will find their spending power falling, while those who can get wage increases in line with or above the inflation rate will not become worse off.

　　A low and stable rate of inflation may produce enough stability and buoyancy to benefit the economy when it comes to promoting economic growth and achieving full employment, whereas accelerating inflation may have exactly the opposite effect. As it distorts markets, so it will slow rates of economic growth and cause the level of unemployment to rise, particularly if it leads to industrial disputes and conflicts in labour markets.

　　If the rate of inflation is the same as in other countries, it is likely that there will be no effect on the balance of payments. If the rate is lower than its trading partners, the exchange rate may rise. If it is accelerating, it is likely to be above the rate in other countries and this will cause a current account deficit that is likely to lead to a fall in the external value of the currency.

ⓔ **7/10 marks awarded.** Good points are covered and there is some recognition that the effects will vary.

(e) The government has four main macroeconomic policy objectives. They are to maintain a high level of employment, a low stable rate of inflation, a satisfactory balance of payments and a growing economy. What is meant by the question is that pursuit of any one of these policy objectives may have a damaging effect on another policy target.

　　If the government tried to raise aggregate demand to increase employment, it may also encourage growth, but cause the rate of inflation to rise and the current balance on the balance of payments to move into deficit.

If the government tried to reduce inflation by reducing aggregate demand, then this may benefit the external account, but worsen the chances of economic growth and cause unemployment to rise.

Yes, fiscal policy can be used independently from monetary policy. Fiscal policy is how the government affects aggregate demand by changing the balance between revenue from taxation and government expenditure. A budget deficit means that expenditure exceeds taxation and is therefore expansionary, while a budget surplus can be used to dampen down demand.

Monetary policy is concerned with the ways that the government can expand the economy by increasing the money supply and/or reducing interest rates.

e **9/18 marks awarded.** The quality of written communication in this answer is good and achieves maximum marks, but some other marks were lost for not fully developing the answer, and the student has not responded to the word 'discuss' in the question. The explanation of how fiscal and monetary policy are used is correct, but there is no indication that the student is aware of the impact that a change in, say, fiscal policy could have on monetary policy and vice versa.

e **Scored 37/60   62% = Grade C**

Question 5 **The UK: is it facing another recession?**

Time allowed: 1 hour 30 minutes

Read the case study below. There are quality of written communication marks in (f) only and it should be answered in continuous prose.

Total marks allocated: 60

Table 1 The UK economy

	2007	2009	2011
Interest rates (%)	5.5	1.0	0.5
Growth (%)	2.6	−4.9	1.1
Inflation (%)	2.3	2.1	4.6
Unemployment (m)	1.65	2.49	2.64
Current account balance (£bn)	−57.8	−18.4	−37.16
Budget deficit (£bn)	39.4	159.8	142.6
National debt (£bn)	618	754	977

In 2008 a series of problems faced by the USA were about to turn toxic for the rest of the world: lending money to potential householders to buy property they could not afford, creating debts that they could not service was to bring about the downfall of Lehman Brothers and cause a crisis in bank lending that led to monetary contractions across the world.

In the UK the threat of recession in 2009 caused the Bank of England to respond by reducing the base interest rate and attempting to kickstart the economy by introducing a quantitative easing programme that expanded the amount of cash in the economy by £200 billion. At the same time the Treasury and government planned an expansionary fiscal policy to boost growth and employment.

By 2010 it was clear that the usual economic levers were not having the expected effect and recovery was not apparent. This led the government, the Bank of England and the Treasury to consider ways in which they could protect the economy from a double-dip recession.

(a) (i) Explain the main components of the trade cycle.   (4 marks)

(ii) Identify and explain two statistics in Table 1 that suggest a recession is imminent.   (4 marks)

ⓔ Both parts are worth 4 marks so take that into account when developing your answers.

(b) (i) What is the difference between the budget deficit and the national debt?   (2 marks)

(ii) What are the main ways in which unemployment is measured?   (4 marks)

ⓔ You are looking for one main distinguishing feature in part (i) and two main measures in part (ii).

(c) Identify the main macroeconomic policies that can be used to manage the economy. (8 marks)

ⓔ There are four main macroeconomic policies — you should include all four in your answer.

(d) (i) Why does the balance of payments always have a zero balance? (2 marks)
(ii) Why is a current balance deficit a potential problem for an economy? (4 marks)
(iii) Which options are available to reduce the size of a current balance deficit? (6 marks)

ⓔ Do not confuse the external account referred to in these questions with the internal budget account.

(e) Explain how monetary policy can be used to expand an economy. (8 marks)

ⓔ Use both price of money and quantity of money in your explanation.

(f) Discuss the ways in which the level of unemployment can be reduced and suggest which solution is least likely to aggravate inflation. (18 marks)

ⓔ You need to reflect on the debate about the effectiveness of the different approaches to reducing unemployment.

Mark scheme

(a) (i) Recession and recovery are mentioned in the text and boom and depression make up the cycle. For identifying the terms (3 marks) and the correct sequence (1 mark).

(ii) Any two of: interest rates being reduced because of concern about a forthcoming recession, large budget deficits, growth below target, unemployment rising and/or a large current balance deficit (4 marks).

(b) (i) In order to achieve 2 marks it is necessary to recognise that the budget deficit is measured over 1 year while the national debt accumulates over many years.

(ii) An explanation of the claimant count (2 marks) and the labour force survey (2 marks).

(c) Identification of fiscal policy (2 marks), monetary policy (2 marks), exchange rate policy (2 marks) and supply-side policies (2 marks).

(d) (i) Show how any imbalances on the current and capital accounts will be offset by official financing on the financial account to produce a zero balance (2 marks).

(ii) It suggests the currency is overvalued and means that a country is not selling enough of its products abroad to finance the required purchase of imports (4 marks).

(iii) Reference can be made to deflationary macroeconomic policies, depreciation of the exchange rate, tariffs, quotas, subsidies, regulations to restrict imports (6 marks).

(e) An explanation of monetary policy and how it is used to expand the economy (8 marks).

(f) Expect an explanation and discussion of the various demand-side policies including monetary, fiscal and exchange rate, and supply-side policies including attempts to increase market freedom, improve incentives and promote developments in productivity, followed by a conclusion that supply-side policies are least likely to aggravate inflation (14 marks + 4 marks for quality of written communication).

A-grade answer

(a) (i) In 2011 the UK economy was described as in recession with output not growing and unemployment rising. This could lead to a depression which is the lowest point in the cycle. From here the economy may begin a recovery phase as growth and employment pick up and may peak out with a boom phase where growth is high and unemployment low.

🅮 **4/4 marks awarded.** This answer scores full marks as the student has identified each of the phases and placed them in a correct sequence.

    (ii) Unemployment has continued to rise and the current account deficit is growing suggesting that domestic production is not picking up.

🅮 **2/4 marks awarded.**

(b) (i) The budget deficit refers to the government policy of spending more than it receives in tax and the national debt is what it has borrowed.

🅮 **1/2 marks awarded.** This does not make it clear that one is a yearly debt and the other is cumulative.

    (ii) The claimant count is a more precise calculation of those registering as unemployed while the labour force survey is an estimate of all those available, but not currently working.

🅮 **4/4 marks awarded.** Full marks: 2 marks for identifying the two measures and 2 marks for the brief explanation of each.

(c) There are four main macroeconomic policies. The first is fiscal policy which manages the economy through the balance between government expenditure and taxation. A deficit is used to expand the economy and a surplus to slow excessive price rises. Monetary policy is expansionary when interest rates are reduced and quantitative easing takes place, while a rise in interest rates would be considered contractionary. The economy can be managed by a number of supply-side policies which are not aimed at changing the overall level of aggregate demand, but are aimed at making the economy more efficient and flexible in its various component parts for products and productive factors.

🅮 **6/8 marks awarded.** The answer identifies that there are four policies but fails to identify or explain the fourth.

(d) (i) Any deficits or surpluses on the account will be matched by an opposite flow of funds from official financing thus producing a zero balance.

🅮 **2/2 marks awarded.**

(ii) The current account produces a balance between the value of exported and imported goods and services. A deficit means the UK is not selling enough products to finance its purchase of imports. If this continues it means the currency value on foreign exchange markets is too high. If this persists then action will be required to deflate the economy or depreciate the currency.

🄴 **3/4 marks awarded.**

(iii) A current balance deficit could be reduced by a deflationary policy which would reduce demand for imports and domestic products, and would therefore release more products to sell abroad. Depreciating or devaluing the exchange rate will make exports cheaper and imports more expensive. Tariffs placed on certain imports or all imports will raise tax for the government and reduce consumption while quotas will limit the volume of imports.

🄴 **5/6 marks awarded.** A few other options could have been considered.

(e) Suppose it was necessary to use monetary policy to expand aggregate monetary demand. Basically there are two ways of expanding monetary demand.

First, the Monetary Policy Committee of the Bank of England can decide to lower interest rates. This can have two expansionary effects. It can encourage more investment in capital, as it becomes more profitable for firms to borrow and expand their productive capacity, or it can encourage consumers to increase their borrowing, particularly to purchase higher-priced consumer durables. However, neither of these things are guaranteed to take place if interest rates are lowered.

The second approach is directly to expand the money supply to boost government expenditure and in this case a part of the public sector borrowing requirement will be financed by printing money. While this technique boosts demand, it may also have damaging effects on the rate of inflation in the economy. If it is considered necessary to contract monetary demand, then interest rates can be raised and overfunding can remove money from circulation.

Either approach may not have the desired effect, as it could be that inflation and exchange rates may be adversely affected. For example, an attempt to boost aggregate monetary demand may cause more imports to be demanded and potential exports to be sold off in the domestic market, leading to a deterioration in the balance of payments.

🄴 **7/8 marks awarded.** This is a good attempt at explaining how monetary policy works.

(f) In the past, fiscal policy was considered to be the most potent policy for curing high levels of unemployment. A high level of unemployment was considered to be a waste of productive capacity and likely to be the result of a deficient level of aggregate demand. In order to boost demand, the government can budget for a deficit. This can be done by lowering taxes and keeping expenditure constant, or raising expenditure and holding taxes constant. This will shift the aggregate demand curve to the right, as illustrated below.

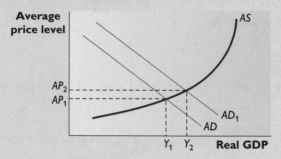

The level of real GDP will rise to Y_2 and there would be some inflation if the AS curve is upward sloping from left to right and prices rise from AP_1 to AP_2. As the *AD* curve shifts right so there comes a point where the level of employment is at its highest and inflation would accelerate if demand continued to increase.

A similar policy that can be used to boost aggregate monetary demand is monetary policy. Here a reduction in the 14-day gilt repo rate (the bank rate) will transmit itself throughout the banking system into lower borrowing rates. This will increase the demand for credit money and expand the overall demand for goods and services. As labour is a derived demand, more people will be employed to produce more products.

Another way to increase demand for UK products is to allow the exchange rate to depreciate. This will make exports cheaper and increase foreign demand, as well as increasing the price of imports. The rise in the price of imports will encourage domestic consumers to demand more UK products. This will boost demand for labour in the UK.

There is some debate among economists about the shape of the aggregate supply curve and it is possible that it is vertical, as illustrated in the following diagram.

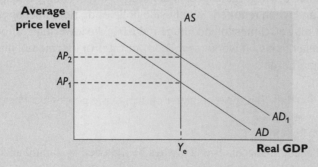

In this case, a shift from *AD* to AD_1 will only result in inflation, and therefore, in order to increase employment, it is necessary to use supply-side policies to shift the AS curve to the right. This means making product and labour markets more competitive, lowering income and corporation taxes to motivate workers and firms and carrying out retraining of labour as new skills are demanded by firms.

Overall, it is supply-side policies that are least likely to cause inflation, as they are directly concerned with increasing productivity and output and do not depend upon an increase in aggregate monetary demand in order to create new jobs.

(e) **15/18 marks awarded.** This is a good answer that is well written and scores full marks for quality of written communication. There is also relevant discussion of the strengths and weaknesses of the various policies that can be used to increase employment.

Scored 49/60   82% = Grade A

C-grade answer

(a) (i) The trade cycle refers to the ups and downs of the business cycle from boom to bust.

(e) **2/4 marks awarded.** This is a limited description of the top and bottom of the cycle.

(ii) The large budget deficit is caused because unemployment is rising and tax is falling while government expenditure has to increase to cover the welfare payments to the unemployed.

(e) **4/4 marks awarded.**

(b) (i) The difference is that the national debt grows each year there is a budget deficit.

(e) **2/2 marks awarded.**

(ii) Claimant count and labour force survey.

(e) **2/4 marks awarded.** The student knows the measures but gives no explanation of either.

(c) Exchange rate policy, monetary policy and fiscal policy are demand-side policies which influence the aggregate level of demand in the economy to expand or contract as and when required. Supply-side policies do not affect aggregate demand but may do things to encourage industry like lowering corporation tax or making it easier to lay off workers while lower rates of income tax may encourage people to work harder.

(e) **4/8 marks awarded.** This answer is better on supply-side policies, but does not explain the other policies in any detail.

(d) (i) Current account surpluses will always be matched by capital account surpluses and vice versa.

(e) **2/2 marks awarded.**

(ii) At some point, if a country continues to run a deficit, it will go bankrupt, its currency will lose its value on foreign exchange markets, and its debt will become junk while its credit rating will also be downgraded to junk status.

ⓔ **4/4 marks awarded.** This is an extreme view but it is not incorrect.

> **(iii)** Deflation, devaluation, tariffs, quotas, subsidies, regulations.

ⓔ **2/8 marks awarded.** An unexplained list like this will not achieve a pass mark, but it does show some relevant knowledge.

(e) Monetary policy is using the rate of interest and the quantity of money in the economy to manage the overall level of aggregate demand. It is managed by the Monetary Policy Committee (MPC) of the Bank of England, which meets once a month and usually makes one of three decisions: to leave the bank rate unchanged, to increase or decrease the rate by quarter percent.

    If the MPC wants the economy to expand, then it will lower interest rates. This will filter through the financial sector of the economy and the lower borrowing rates will increase the demand for purchasing on credit. Overall, the increase in aggregate monetary demand will increase the demand for goods and services and the firms that receive increased orders will then employ more factors of production. The government will use this type of policy when unemployment is above the desired level.

    In the past, policies directly used to affect the money supply were used to manage aggregate demand. These included changes in reserve ratios, ceilings on lending and special deposits. Although they are still available to expand the money supply, they are not currently in use, as the Bank of England concentrates solely on adjusting interest rates.

ⓔ **7/8 marks awarded.** This is a clear explanation of how an expansionary monetary policy works.

(f) The level of unemployment can be unacceptably high. For example, in the past unemployment has been as high as nearly one quarter of the workforce or as low as 2%. Facing this considerable difference, governments have taken it upon themselves to try to manage the economy to a stable high level of employment.

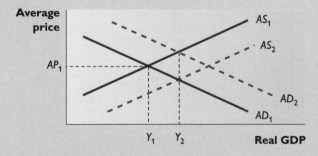

    In the diagram above we can assume that Y_1 is the current equilibrium level of employment, but Y_2 has been achievable in the past and may be achievable now. Given this information, there are two ways to move from Y_1 to Y_2. Either the aggregate demand curve can be shifted to the right by expansionary fiscal and/or

> monetary policies, or the lowering of the exchange rate, or the aggregate supply curve could be shifted to the right using supply-side policies. It is these supply-side policies that are least likely to aggravate inflation.

🅮 **10/18 marks awarded.** This is a well-constructed and well-written answer with all the main points included. However, there is not sufficient detail to achieve a higher mark. For example, fiscal and monetary policy are referred to, but neither is explained.

🅮 **Scored 39/60   65% = Grade C**

Question 6 Changing expenditure patterns

Time allowed: 1 hour 30 minutes

Read the case study below. There are quality of written communication marks in (e) only and it should be answered in continuous prose.

Total marks allocated: 60

The statistics in Table 1 below indicate that since 2004 there have been significant changes in the components of expenditure that make up the UK's gross domestic product. The government has tried, in its expenditure plans, to avoid crowding out the private sector and recognised the importance of the multiplier effect of investment on the economy. There is evidence that more is being produced to be shared among a steadily growing population.

Table 1 Expenditure and the gross domestic product (constant prices 2003 £m)

	Consumer spending	Government spending	Investment	Exports	Imports	GDP	Population size (000s)	GDP/ capita
2004	709,702	227,424	181,506	290,989	332,953		59,846	
2005	722,866	232,094	187,539	305,991	348,914		60,238	
2006	745,737	250,630	215,985	358,356	394,789		60,587	
2007	768,397	253,315	229,423	339,434	383,162		60,793	

(a) (i) Define GDP and calculate the figures that should appear in the columns for GDP and GDP per capita in Table 1. (4 marks)
  (ii) Which component of GDP showed the largest percentage change between 2004 and 2007? (1 mark)
  (iii) What are the three ways of measuring GDP? Identify one problem associated with each measurement. (6 marks)
  (iv) The statistics in Table 1 are measured at 'constant prices 2003'. What does this mean and, therefore, what changes are being illustrated in the table? (3 marks)

ℯ Make careful use of the statistics where appropriate.

(b) (i) Which component of GDP is likely to accelerate the rate of economic growth? Explain your choice. (3 marks)
  (ii) Identify the percentage change in 'government spending' and 'investment' for the period 2004–07. (2 marks)
  (iii) What is 'crowding out'? Does the answer to b (ii) suggest that crowding out has taken place? (4 marks)

ℯ Your answers need to make clear references to Table 1 where appropriate.

(c) (i) Between 2004 and 2007, compare the overall change in 'consumer spending' with that of 'investment'. (2 marks)

(ii) What are the main determinants of:
- consumer spending?
- investment? (4 marks)

(iii) 'Changes in investment have a multiplier effect on GDP.' What does this statement mean? (4 marks)

(e) There are a number of economic concepts to analyse in your answers.

(d) What are the advantages and disadvantages to an economy of having a high proportion of its GDP determined by the flow of imports and exports? (9 marks)

(e) Include both positives and negatives in your answer.

(e) Discuss whether there should be more or less government intervention in the macroeconomic management of the economy. (18 marks)

(e) You may agree with more or less government intervention, but you must evaluate both views to access the full range of marks.

Mark scheme

(a) (i) Expect a definition in terms of expenditure income or output (2 marks). For a correct set of GDP figures (1 mark) and GDP per capita (1 mark).

	GDP (£m)	GDP/capita
2004	1,076,668	17,990
2005	1,099,576	18,254
2006	1,175,919	19,409
2007	1,207,407	19,861

(ii) Investment + 26.4% (1 mark).

(iii) Income (1 mark), output (1 mark), expenditure (1 mark), plus one example of a problem for each, e.g. self-provided products for income (1 mark), double counting for output (1 mark), changes in the value of money for expenditure (1 mark).

(iv) All components of GDP are measured as if the prices are fixed at the 2003 level (1 mark). This removes any distortion caused by changes in the value of money (1 mark) and therefore shows changes in output or real GDP (1 mark).

(b) (i) It is most likely that investment (1 mark) will be chosen, although a reasoned case can be made for other variables. An explanation of the relationship between investment and economic growth (2 marks).

(ii) Government spending, 11.4% (1 mark); investment, 26.4% (1 mark).

(iii) Explain crowding out (2 marks) and explain how if government spending rises significantly more slowly than investment, then crowding out is probably not taking place (2 marks).

(c) (i) Consumer spending rose by 8.3%, whereas investment rose more than three times as fast at 26.4% (2 marks).

(ii) Expect at least a sentence to explain the determinants of consumer spending to include such things as disposable income, level and rate of change of income, attitude towards saving and spending, distribution of income, structure of population, interest rates etc. (2 marks), and for investment expect such things as interest rates, business confidence, expectations, government policy, marginal efficiency of investment etc. (2 marks).

(iii) Expect reference to investment being an injection into the circular flow of income and a description of how an injection of a certain amount will bring about successive rises in income, such that the final change in income is greater than the initial change (4 marks).

(d) The answer should explain the advantages of a high proportion of international trade, including greater variety, more efficient allocation of resources, higher real incomes, greater interdependence. For disadvantages, the answer should include dependency on foreign traders, significant risk of dumping, less stable exchange rate, strategic problems, disruption to supply etc. (9 marks).

(e) There are various ways of answering this question. For example, a student may take each of the macroeconomic problems and evaluate the degree to which more or less involvement may produce benefits. Alternatively, a comparison of the views regarding the weaknesses of capitalism and the need for governments to compensate in the form of demand management, or a recognition of the strengths of capitalism and the need for governments to withdraw from active management and encourage free markets and competition (14 marks + 4 marks for quality of written communication).

A-grade answer

(a) (i) GDP is gross domestic product, which is a measure of how much is produced in an economy over a given period of time. The GDP figures are calculated from the equation $GDP = C + G + I + X - M$. Therefore:

$$2004 = 1,076,668$$
$$2005 = 1,099,576$$
$$2006 = 1,175,919$$
$$2007 = 1,207,407$$

The GDP per capita is GDP divided by the total population:

$$2004 = 17,990$$
$$2005 = 18,254$$
$$2006 = 19,409$$
$$2007 = 19,861$$

e 4/4 marks awarded.

(ii) Investment changes the most, increasing by 26.4%.

e 1/1 mark awarded.

(iii) The economy can be measured by adding up all the expenditure over a period of time and, where inflation is a problem, this needs to be removed in order to identify real changes. Alternatively, the output of all the firms can be added together. To avoid double counting, it is necessary to measure only the value added by each firm. The final measure is to add up everyone's income, while recognising the problem that people do not always provide correct information about their income.

e 6/6 marks awarded.

(iv) The product of the economy is measured as if prices never change from the 2003 figures. The result of this is that the figures show real changes in output rather than nominal changes in the value of money.

e 3/3 marks awarded.

(b) (i) Investment is the purchase of capital in the form of new machines and factories. Increases in this area of expenditure are likely to boost the productive potential of the economy.

e 3/3 marks awarded.

(ii) Government spending rose by 11.4%, which is less than investment, which rose by 26.4%.

e 2/2 marks awarded.

(iii) Crowding out is when government spending — particularly when financed by public-sector borrowing and higher interest rates — restricts private investment and consumption. The statistics in the question do not give conclusive support to this statement, as the increase in government expenditure is matched by the even larger increase in investment.

e 4/4 marks awarded.

(c) (i) Investment rose by 26.4%, which is slightly more than three times the rise in consumer spending, which grew by 8.27%.

e 2/2 marks awarded.

(ii) The level of consumer spending in the economy depends upon the rate of interest. Lower rates encourage more borrowing. Also the level of a person's income affects their spending pattern. Arguably, higher income leads to more spending, though the marginal propensity to consume may fall at higher levels of income. Investment is determined by the rate of interest and the marginal efficiency of capital investment, i.e. the return on capital.

ⓔ **2/4 marks awarded.** The answer only deals with two points for consumer spending and two for investment.

(iii) Investment is an injection into the circular flow of income. Because income is created through the process of derived demand, then the total effect on income will be greater than the original change in investment.

ⓔ **3/4 marks awarded.** This answer is a little too brief for full marks.

(d) If a high proportion of GDP is determined by international trade and this trade is due to free trade without barriers, then economic theory tells us that absolute advantage and comparative advantage will produce gains from trade. This is likely to mean that standards of living will be higher than if a country had little international trade because of protective barriers. The high level of free international trade should produce a more efficient allocation of resources and higher real incomes.

A greater exposure to international trade increases the variety of products available to the consumer. Also, the increased competition between firms worldwide drives prices down and improves the quality of products on the market.

In contrast, a high dependency on imports can make a country vulnerable to things outside its control. For example, one country may be able to threaten another country at a diplomatic level or even talk about war if it has control of supply over a vital resource like food.

Dependency on foreign firms may also damage a firm or whole industry if supply of important raw materials or components is interrupted by strike action, which is outside the control of the domestic economy. Similarly, political decisions may be made in one country that significantly affect the flow of imports and exports to the host country. This may deprive consumers of the choice they previously had.

ⓔ **7/9 marks awarded.** This is a well-written answer with a good range of points.

(e) The history of government intervention in the UK economy is one of an ever-increasing amount. This has raised a question among economists regarding the level of government involvement. Traditionally, Keynesian economists have argued that the economy has weak self-regulatory powers and therefore government must maintain control over the aggregate level of demand in the economy. At the other extreme are more liberal economists, who argue that the state is stifling competition and enterprise and should therefore reduce its involvement in the economy.

The argument for intervention is based upon the assumption that, because of inherent weaknesses in the capitalist system, the economy is likely to stumble through periods of depression and high unemployment to booming growth followed by accelerating inflation. In order to stabilise the economy at full employment, it is necessary to budget for a deficit and boost aggregate demand when there is a slump in economic activity and rising unemployment. Alternatively, when there is accelerating inflation, the government will need to budget for a surplus and dampen down the level of aggregate demand. This intervention in managing the economy requires both monetary and fiscal policy to be active participants in maintaining a growing economy that uses all its resources in a full and sustainable way.

Other economists have been critical of this interventional approach, saying that governments do not have enough information about how to manage an economy efficiently and hence their attempts at macroeconomic management have tended to lead to excessive inflation, higher than expected unemployment and a weak fluctuating external currency. They tend to argue that government should run a balanced budget and pursue a steady, slow growth in the money supply roughly in line with the growth in output. On the supply side of the economy, the government needs only to ensure that firms remain competitive and that profits remain as a reward for enterprise, and a signal to move resources to where profits are strong, and away from areas where profits are declining or losses are being incurred.

Overall, it does seem that in recent years the government has moved towards less macroeconomic management; the Bank of England has been made independent (1997) and given an inflation target of 2%. This emphasis on monetary policy has limited the ability of government to use its fiscal policy in a counter-cyclical way. However, the government still spends a large proportion of the national income and it may be that the tax burden is a greater issue for discussion than more or less macroeconomic management.

(e) **16/18 marks awarded.** This is a good answer. It is well written, achieving maximum marks for quality of written communication, and has a strong discussion running through it.

(e) **Scored 53/60   88% = Grade A**

C-grade answer

(a) (i) GDP is C + G + I + X − M.
  2004 = 1,076,668; 2005 = 1,099,576; 2006 = 1,175,919; 2007 = 1,207,407.
  GDP per capita is per person, therefore:
  2004 = 17,990; 2005 = 18,254; 2006 = 19,409; 2007 = 19,861.

(e) **3/4 marks awarded.** The answer needs to include a little more detail on GDP, i.e. a measure of domestic output over a period of time.

  (ii) Consumer spending rises by £58,695 from £709,702 to £768,397.

ⓔ **0/1 mark awarded.** The question asks for the largest percentage change.

> **(iii)** The three ways of measuring GDP are income, output and expenditure, and three problems are difficulties of collecting statistics, the black market (where unrecorded transactions take place) and inflation.

ⓔ **5/6 marks awarded.** The student loses 1 mark for not relating the problems identified to a particular measure, as the question asks.

> **(iv)** Constant prices mean the prices that existed in 2003 and therefore the statistics do not include inflation.

ⓔ **2/3 marks awarded.** This answer is almost there, but in order to get the third mark the student should have made a reference to 'real' or 'output'.

> **(b) (i)** A rise in exports injects spending into the circular flow of income and this in turn boosts aggregate demand and stimulates economic growth.

ⓔ **2/3 marks awarded.** The student did not choose investment, but makes out a reasonable case for exports. However, the impact of exports is more likely to be on growth in output than a growth in productive potential.

> **(ii)** Between 2004 and 2007 government spending rises by a few percent and investment rises a lot.

ⓔ **0/2 marks awarded.** The student is asked for percentages and seems not to know how to calculate them.

> **(iii)** Crowding out is where the public sector interferes in the private sector of the economy. Crowding out could have happened between 2004 and 2007 because the government was spending a lot more money.

ⓔ **0/4 marks awarded.** This is uninspired guesswork.

> **(c) (i)** The overall change in consumer spending was a rise of £58,695m, while the increase in investment was only £47,917m. This means that consumer spending has grown faster than investment.

ⓔ **0/2 marks awarded.** The student has not realised that the comparative change is the other way round if one looks at the rate of change rather than the raw totals, i.e. investment is growing at twice the rate of consumer spending.

(ii) The main determinants of consumer spending are the consumers' income, their attitude to spending and saving and how much money they can borrow at a specific interest rate. The main determinants of investment are again the rate of interest, how fast the economy is growing and how profitable a new investment may be in the future.

ⓔ **4/4 marks awarded.**

(iii) When a government decides to invest in a new motorway, lots of people will be employed and paid an income. They in turn will go to the shops and spend their income on food and drink etc. With the money they spend in the shops, the shopkeeper can go out and buy more things and so it goes on. This means that the final effect on everyone's income is much greater than the original amount of money invested in producing the new motorway, and GDP rises by a multiple of the original change.

ⓔ **4/4 marks awarded.** This is a simplistic — but correct — description of how the multiplier works, so this answer scores full marks.

(d) The advantages of GDP making up a high proportion of international trade are likely to be a greater variety of products available to the consumer and higher real standards of living, as the trade is likely to have been the result of countries specialising in the products for which they have the lower opportunity cost. This will lead to gains from trade compared with a lack of specialisation and division of labour.

However, there are disadvantages when one country relies upon another country, especially if it is for important items like foodstuffs and defence products. Also, when there are large fluctuations in international trade, they may bring about changes in economic activity that cannot be controlled domestically by government intervention. A high level of imports could result from dumping, and this is likely to damage domestic producers, as they will be competing with firms from other countries who are selling below their costs of production.

ⓔ **5/9 marks awarded.** This answer contains a number of relevant points, but its coverage is fairly superficial.

(e) Governments intervene in the economy to manage the macroeconomic problems of high unemployment, high inflation, balance of payment disequilibrium and low or no economic growth.

In the past, the main thrust of macroeconomic management was to use fiscal policies, monetary policies and exchange rate policies to manipulate aggregate demand. This fine tuning is aimed at stabilising the economy at a full employment equilibrium. The pursuit of this type of demand-side policy was a recognition that capitalism had weak self-regulatory mechanisms and could settle at high levels of unemployment over sustained periods of time.

For a period of time after the Second World War these policies seemed to be successful, but in the seventies and eighties it became obvious that governments were not able to reconcile the big economic problems.

Over recent years, there has been a different approach to economic management which has meant less intervention by government. Government no longer talks about full employment targets and has made an independent Bank of England responsible for achieving an inflation target. It seems that government has recognised the benefits of not interfering in a market economy and many state-run industries have been returned to the private sector. Government has been most concerned to encourage competition and to motivate workers and firms into becoming more productive.

There are strong opinions on both sides of this argument, but it does seem that at this point in time the argument for less government intervention is in the ascendancy.

ⓔ **15/18 marks awarded.** This is a well-written answer, achieving 4 marks for quality of written communication. It makes some attempt at a conclusion.

ⓔ **Scored 40/60   67% = Grade C**

Knowledge check answers

1 The AS curve is shifted to the right by reductions in the cost of production, increases in the quantity of productive factors and improvements in the quality of performance by productive factors.

2 Figure 1 (b) as in some theoretical descriptions of aggregate supply the condition is described as flexible in the short run to changes in aggregate demand, but inflexible or non-responsive in the long run.

3 Fiscal and monetary policies are both demand management policies.

4 Boosting demand may damage the economy by increasing the rate of inflation or worsening the current account of the balance of payments.

5 Supply-side policies include deregulation of an overburdened industry, privatisation, promotion of fair competition, reinforcement of private property rights, changes in marginal tax rates and improved employee training among many other things. Overall these are not designed to change the fiscal balance between expenditure and taxation and therefore they are not classed as demand-side policies.

6 An expansionary fiscal policy is when the government budgets for a deficit by increasing government spending without a corresponding increase in tax or when it cuts taxation without cutting spending, or a combination of both.

7 It is the demand for imports that determines the supply of domestic currency, while the demand for exports determines the demand for that currency.

8 Domestic production is originally at Q_1 without international trade. It is reduced to Q_5 when free trade becomes international.

9 (a) The Bank of England was given independence from political control in 1997.

(b) The euro was first adopted in 1999.

Page numbers in **bold** refer to **key term definitions**

A

absolute advantage 17, 19

aggregate demand 8, 9–11, 16, 18, 42

aggregate demand curve 9–10, 11, 16, 19, 42

aggregate monetary demand 16, 18

aggregate supply 8, 9–11

aggregate supply curve 9–10, 11, 16, 19, 42

AS/AD model 11, 20

B

balance of payments 12, **13**, 14, 32, 62

balance of trade 32

Bank of England 16, 61

budget deficit 61

C

circular flow of income 9, 10, **11**, 42

Claimant Count 13

closed economies 17

comparative advantage 17, 19, 20

competition 16

constant prices 69

consumer expenditure 9, 70

consumer price index (CPI) 12, 14

contractionary fiscal/monetary policies 16, 17

credit crunch **16**

crowding out 69

current account of balance of payments 12, 13, 14, 17

current balance deficit/surplus 32, 62

D

demand-side policies 15, 18, 19, 20, 42

deregulation 16

differential tax rates 17

disposable income 42

dumping **17**, 20

E

economic growth **13**, 14, 17, 24, 42, 51, 69

economic recession 32, 33, 61–68

Ethiopia 23–31

euro 51–60

European Union 18, 19, 51

Eurozone measures 12, 51, 52

exchange rate policies 14, 16, 18, 33, 52

expansionary fiscal policy 15, 16

expansionary monetary policy 16, 32

expenditure 13, 14, 69–77

exports 9, 18, 70

external costs 14

external debt per person 24

F

financial account 14

fiscal policy 14, 16, 18, 20, 32, 42, 52

foreign exchange market 23

free market 52

free trade 17, 19, 33

G

gains from trade 17, 20

General Agreement on Tariffs and Trade (GATT) 18

general equilibrium 9, 11, 42

government economic policy objectives 8, 12–15

government expenditure 9, 16, 69

government intervention 11, 24, 70

gross domestic product (GDP) 13, 14, 23, 24, 69, 70

growth rates 12, 13, 14, 24, 52

H

harmonised index of consumer prices (HICP) 12

human development index (HDI) 24

I

imports 9, 18, 70

income 13, 14

index numbers 14

individual cost 14

infant industries 17, 20

inflation 12, 14, 16, 24, 51, 52, 62

injections 9, 10, 11, 42